HENRY V

POCKET
GIANTS

HENRY V

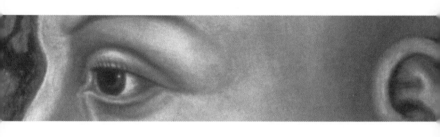

POCKET
GIANTS

A.J. POLLARD

The
History
Press

For Magnus, another pocket giant

Cover image © The Bridgeman Art Library

First published 2014

The History Press
The Mill, Brimscombe Port
Stroud, Gloucestershire, GL5 2QG
www.thehistorypress.co.uk

British Library Cataloguing in Publication Data.
A catalogue record for this book is available from the British Library.

ISBN 978 0 7524 9763 1

Typesetting and origination by The History Press
Printed in Europe

Contents

Introduction

'His deeds exceed all speech'[1]

It snowed heavily the day Henry V was crowned: 9 April, Palm Sunday, 1413. Writing a few years later, Thomas Walsingham, the resident chronicler at St Albans abbey, recalled two interpretations of this unseasonable weather. Some thought it portended that the new king would be cold hearted and rule his subjects harshly; others took it as an omen that vice would be frozen and new virtues would flourish in the coming spring. In the event, as Walsingham surely intended his readers to understand, both were right. Henry proved to be a cold-hearted, ruthless monarch, yet his rule also represented a new beginning and gave his nation fresh hope after the troubled reigns of his predecessors.

This King of England, whose reign had such a chilly start, was a giant of his age. Not simply because he was a great and famous warrior and a paragon of military virtue. He was a giant because he imposed himself on his contemporaries. He was feared, famed and respected by all, his enemies as well as his friends. He truly bestrode his world.

Thanks to Shakespeare, Henry V is the best-known military hero in English history; more famous even than Marlborough or Wellington, let alone his mighty great-grandfather, King Edward III, who reigned for over fifty years. He enjoyed more success against the French, the ancient enemy, than any of them, coming tantalisingly close to conquering that vast country and imposing an English dynasty. He did this in a reign of just nine years, seven years of which he was at war. Even before he died at the tender age of 35, the myth of his greatness was being created, and it was further honed in subsequent decades. Shakespeare's play has become the touchstone of English national pride, English courage and English imperialism. For good or ill, Henry V embodies the military might of England.

He was a remarkably successful soldier, yet his warrior skills were not always deployed in the best interests of his kingdom, let alone the people of Wales or France who suffered at his hands. Serious questions arise concerning his judgement. Was a war of conquest in France really sustainable? Did he damage his own realm in pursuit of foreign glory? Was he truly a figure of Christian piety and virtue? Or did there lie behind the carefully constructed chivalric image, a cold, calculating and manipulative autocrat?

These are some of the questions this book explores. It seeks to explain why Henry V was so successful, so admired and so idolised. But this is not another exercise in hero-worship. There is no doubt that Henry V was an awe-inspiring man, a charismatic leader, an astute politician, a gifted administrator and a brilliant general. However, Thomas Walsingham's hope of a new beginning was to prove an illusion, and the tragic legacy of Henry's nine hectic years on the throne was embroilment in an unwinnable war and domestic problems stored for the future.

1

'So blest a son': Childhood and Youth, 1386–1406[2]

Henry V was born at Monmouth on 16 September 1386. He was not expected to become king. But he was in direct line of succession to the throne, as great-grandson of King Edward III, grandson of John of Gaunt, Duke of Lancaster, and eldest son of Henry of Bolingbroke, Earl of Derby. The house of Lancaster was the most powerful in England under the throne and 'Time-honoured' Gaunt was the mightiest of magnates, a European prince and by far the king's richest subject, with hundreds of lords and knights retained in his service throughout the realm. Bolingbroke, Henry's father, was a great noble in his own right and a young man of chivalric renown. He became embroiled in the factional politics of King Richard II's court during Gaunt's absence overseas in the years 1386–89. He then set out himself on foreign ventures, first on crusade to Prussia and then on pilgrimage to the Holy Land between 1390 and 1393.

The boy Henry saw little of his father, but this was not unusual: until the age of 7 noble children were usually cared for in their mother's household. When he later became king, he remembered his nurse, Joan Waryn, to whom he granted an annuity of £20. His mother, Mary Bohun, the joint heiress to the Earldom of Hereford, died in June 1394. What impact her death had on the 7-year-old we do not know, although he commissioned an image for her tomb in the church of St Mary de Castro in Leicester on his accession to the throne. Throughout his life he remained close to his maternal grandmother, Joan, the dowager countess who almost certainly influenced his religious development.

He may already have moved, when he was 7, to the household of his grandfather for the customary next stage of his upbringing. Here, as well as military training (he attended his first tournament when he was 10) and schooling in the arts of hunting and falconry, he received a liberal education. His tutor was his young uncle Henry Beaufort, later the Cardinal Bishop of Winchester, one of Gaunt's sons by Katherine Swynford. Young Henry was supplied with grammar books and learnt to play the harp. When he was still only 12 he joined the household of King Richard himself – at which point his childhood was dramatically and prematurely brought to an end.

In normal times, entering the royal household would have been unexceptional. But times were far from normal. In 1398 Henry's father, Bolingbroke, had clashed with the king and had been exiled for ten years. Gaunt had secured an undertaking that, should he die, his heir, now Duke of Hereford, would be able to enter his vast Lancastrian inheritance. After Gaunt's death in 1399, the king broke his promise and took the estates into his own hands. Bolingbroke, in Paris, made immediate plans to return to England to recover his right. Richard II, who must surely have anticipated such a reaction, nevertheless pressed on with an expedition to Ireland. With him he took young Henry of Monmouth, to whom he had granted an annuity of £500. Later it was said that a personal bond developed between man and boy, Richard taking the emotional place left vacant by an absent and distant father.

Richard II left the kingdom in charge of his uncle, the Duke of York. He was still in Ireland when Bolingbroke landed at Ravenspur on the coast of Yorkshire. Bolingbroke claimed that he had returned only to recover his rightful inheritance and reform the misgovernnment of the realm. In this he received considerable support, not only from his own and his late father's numerous Lancastrian followers, but also from neutrals such as the powerful Earl of Northumberland. When, a week or two later, Richard II hurriedly returned to North Wales, Henry was already, in effect, in command of the kingdom. The Duke of York had defected; Bristol had fallen; and Chester, the heartland of Ricardian loyalty, had been secured against the king. The Earl of Northumberland was sent to meet the outnumbered monarch at Conwy and Richard was taken into custody.

Bolingbroke and his advisers judged that it was better to hazard usurpation than face the certainty of eventual failure if he forced his rule on a vengeful king. Thus, on 30 September 1399, Richard II 'abdicated' and a new king, calling himself Henry IV, assumed the throne. Despite repeated assurances that Bolingbroke only wished to see reform of the government and that the imprisoned former king would come to no harm, he was dead shortly afterwards.

Henry of Monmouth, who had been left in safekeeping by Richard II in Ireland, returned to England and was reunited with his father, a comparative stranger, in time for the coronation which took place on 13 October. At the ceremony he carried the sword of justice. Two days later he was created Prince of Wales, Duke of Cornwall, Earl of Chester and Duke of Aquitaine – and shortly afterwards granted the additional title of Duke of Lancaster. Over the next year an independent household was established for him, financed by the revenues from Wales, Cornwall and Chester (Henry held only the titles of the other two duchies). By the time of his fourteenth birthday in September 1400 he was treated as a young adult. But of course he was under his father's tutelage.

Henry's military education and training were completed in the field. He had already, in 1399, campaigned under Richard II's wing in Ireland. Now he joined his father with a retinue of over a hundred men under his nominal command on an abortive invasion of Scotland in the summer of 1400. That autumn, a revolt by a leading Welsh landowner, Owain Glyn Dŵr, drew the king, with his son still in his company, into a punitive raid into North Wales. He then installed the English prince in Chester, supported by a council under the leadership of Henry 'Hotspur' Percy, the heir to the Earl of Northumberland. In the spring of 1401, the Welsh rebellion burst into life again. Hotspur, with the prince in his company, secured the important castle town of Conwy, but was unable to prevent the rising against English rule from spreading.

In the autumn of 1402, from his northern mountain sanctuary, Owain was co-ordinating raids throughout the whole of Wales, having declared himself to be the true prince of that land. King Henry IV responded by mounting a three-pronged invasion, with Prince Harry nominally leading an army from Chester. This achieved little other than the relief and revictualling of the North Welsh castles. To add to royal woes, friction developed within the English camp. Hotspur, whose brother-in-law Sir Edmund Mortimer had been captured by the Welsh, was in favour of negotiation and compromise; Henry IV was adamantly against. After a blazing row, Hotspur resigned (or was removed from) his post. On 7 March 1403, the prince was formally sworn in as his father's lieutenant in Wales. He was now in full independent command. His first action was to raid and sack Glyn Dŵr's home at Sycharth. Still only 16, the precocious youth was already a veteran of six campaigns. His grandfather Gaunt had not gone on his first campaign until he was that age; his father not until he was 18.

Henry was shortly to be blooded in a horrific way, in the most ferocious battle fought for decades on English soil. He had been in the saddle frequently since 1399, and had learnt first hand about the rigours of forced marches, the routine revictualling of remote strongholds, the cruelty of plundering raids and the taking of reprisals. But he had yet to fight in a set-piece battle. Now he was pitched into bloody combat against Hotspur, the flower of chivalry. Knowing that Henry IV was marching north on a second Scottish campaign, Percy had hoped to surprise the adolescent prince, link up with Glyn Dŵr and turn on the king. But Henry IV had rapidly diverted and marched back to join his son outside Shrewsbury – just in time to confront Hotspur.

The 16-year-old led the advance against the fearsome Cheshire archers whom Hotspur had recruited to his cause. As he marched forward, Prince Henry was struck by an arrow in his cheek. He broke off the shaft and pressed on without hesitation to engage in the hand-to-hand melee that was a medieval battle. In the end he and his father won the day. The arrow that hit Hotspur killed him; that which hit the prince entered 6 inches into the back of his lower skull – but he survived. The arrow had to be removed by an agonising operation which involved the surgeon devising a special tool to insert and clamp on the head embedded in the bone. Thereafter Henry carried a scar close to his nose. It is not clear how disfigured he was, as it was never referred to publicly, but the scar may explain why, uniquely among English monarchs, his official portrait was made in profile (*see* appendix). After Shrewsbury no one ever doubted his courage and few dared cross the man carrying this mark of honour. His military apprenticeship was complete. War and all that it entailed was etched on his face.

It took Henry well over nine months to recover from his wound; he did not return to active duty until the summer of 1404. By then the whole of Wales was under rebel control and English strategy was restricted to containment. The prince and his household now spent most of their time across the border in Herefordshire. His lieutenants garrisoned the Marcher castles and began slowly to wrest back the initiative. In the early summer of 1405 he was given a renewed command in North Wales as his father's lieutenant, a commission that was regularly extended. But he was beginning to spend time away from the Marches, delegating conduct of the war to deputies. He did not entirely abandon his command; indeed, he had a pressing personal need to recover the principality since it was a major source of his income. But he preferred to lead from a distance, giving priority to ensuring that he received the support he needed – political and financial – from a government hard-pressed from many quarters.

At the beginning of 1406 it was announced that the prince would once again take personal command in Wales and spearhead its reconquest. Parliament was summoned in March to raise funds for the campaign. But in April the king collapsed. He had suffered either a stroke or heart attack. The reconvening of parliament after the Easter recess had to be postponed. Unable to ride, Henry came down from Windsor by boat, but it was immediately apparent that he was seriously incapacitated and not fit enough to govern the kingdom. Thus a continual council was established, its members nominated by parliament, with the king's declared assent to rule in his name. This council was now responsible for bringing royal finances under control. The Commons pressed for firm action.

Prince Henry's reaction to his father's illness, and the possibility of his death, is hard to fathom. In 1404 he had been praised in parliament for his courage and good service in Wales. Now the Commons complained of his continued failure to return to his command. It seems he wanted to be on hand in Westminster since the succession had suddenly become a matter of pressing concern. An act passed in June had confirmed the 19-year-old Prince of Wales as rightful heir to the throne, but its preamble had shown a degree of distrust in him. It openly referred to his 'errors', even as it stressed his good intentions and willingness to be ruled by the council. What lay behind these cryptic remarks, entered formally into the parliamentary record, we do not know. Had the prince perhaps tried to assert his own authority over the royal council?

His Welsh command had been renewed in September, but still Henry did not return to the Marches. Throughout the autumn he seems to have continued to linger in London, where he agitated behind the scenes for a bigger say in government. (There was deadlock between crown and parliament over the terms of reference for the continual council.) Finally, on 8 December 1406, Prince Henry was brought into government to attend his first meeting of the council. His promotion seems to have helped break the deadlock. More sweeping powers to act in the king's name were granted than had been conceded in June. And the Act of Succession, which had offended the prince, was repealed.

Government of the realm was now in the hands of a continual council ruling in the king's name on terms acceptable to the heir to the throne and others who had previously been vocal in parliamentary opposition. A new chancellor, Archbishop Arundel of Canterbury, presided. Parliament was dissolved just before Christmas. For the remaining six years of his father's life, in the context of Henry IV's continuing ill health and fitful capacity to rule, the Prince of Wales was to be a highly visible and active politician.

2

'Riot and dishonour stain the brow': Prince Hal in Politics, 1406–13[3]

For the last six years of Henry IV's reign, Prince Henry was *the* dynamic force in English politics – and an increasingly disruptive one. As the seasons passed, he became more and more frustrated with the restriction of being second in the realm. Like many later Princes of Wales, he became the focus of a faction, which by the end of the reign was in opposition to the king. He made no secret of his belief that he could rule the kingdom better than his enfeebled father. His behaviour in the last years of Henry IV's life made many wonder whether such a headstrong, arrogant and disobedient son was fit to wear the crown.

It all began well enough when the prince joined the continual council. He was an assiduous attender, being present at two-thirds of the recorded meetings in 1407 and even more frequently over the following two years. Tackling the deficit was the major preoccupation of this administration, and, with the king accepting the constraints imposed upon him, the council gradually began to bring the budget under control. The young heir's increasing status is perhaps to be seen in the issuing of a new great seal in which the arms of Prince Henry as Prince of Wales, Duke of Cornwall and Earl of Chester are depicted as supporting those of the king. His influence may also be discerned in the confirmation of the legitimacy of the Beauforts – his half-brothers, John, Earl of Somerset, Henry, Bishop of Winchester, and Sir Thomas – all of whom became close allies.

Having insisted on the necessary financial support, even from a restricted budget, he now did as required. In July he led a well-equipped army to Wales. The objective was to capture Aberystwyth, one of the last remaining strongholds in rebel hands. All went well at first. Terms were agreed for town and castle to surrender on 1 November if Glyn Dŵr failed to relieve them. Confident in the outcome, Henry attended the next parliament which met on 25 October at Gloucester – close to the Marches for his convenience. The Commons were in truculent mood, for they had been assured that no taxation would be needed for two years and members were dissatisfied by the progress made in retrenchment. Nevertheless, before they were dissolved on 2 December, they voted another half subsidy and released the council from its oath to abide by the articles agreed the previous year.

While the prince and some of his senior commanders were thus engaged, however, Glyn Dŵr relieved Aberystwyth. Perhaps because of this failure, and criticism of his conduct of the siege, the prince came before his father to declare, on his knees, his loyalty to him. He also vouched for the faithful service of his cousin, Edward, Duke of York, who had been with his army in Wales. (York, who had succeeded his father in 1400, had been suspected of treason in 1404.) What further suspicion of the prince's behaviour lay behind this unusual submission it is clear that the prince was not trusted by some close to the king, and, it would appear, not even by the king himself. Father and son clashed, as fathers and sons often do. Perhaps the young Henry made no secret of his belief that he could do the job better than his father.

For the following two years the prince was a model subject and dutiful son. In the summer of 1408, he raised another fully financed army, complete with artillery train, and returned once more to Aberystwyth. This time he was successful. His army next moved on to a winter siege of Harlech, while he himself returned to England. His father had become gravely ill. In January 1409 he made his will, and Prince Henry and his younger brother Thomas, who had returned in haste from his command in Ireland, spent several anxious days at his bedside.

To everyone's surprise, the king recovered. But all was far from well. Splits had begun to deepen in the administration. The financial strains were beginning to tell. The supremely self-confident Prince of Wales had absolutely no doubt as to who was best equipped to govern the kingdom in the name of his enfeebled father. He did not feel that reform was being pursued vigorously enough, even though he himself had enjoyed preference from the exchequer for his recent military campaigns. He was also unhappy with the continuing residence of his brother Thomas in England. In May, Thomas was granted £7,000 to cover his arrears as lieutenant in Ireland, whereas Henry received only small allocations for Wales. Prince Henry made it known, with some hypocrisy considering his own earlier dilatoriness, that his brother should leave court and return to his post across the water. He did not. In August Henry attempted to have him removed from office. It was by now apparent that Thomas was their father's favoured son and that there was deep ill feeling between the siblings. Henry may well have believed that Thomas was turning the king and the chancellor against him.

In response, Prince Henry continued to build up a powerful following both on the council and more widely in the realm. As well as the Beauforts, many of his companions in arms in Wales were devoted supporters, especially the Earls of Arundel and Warwick. A coterie of young aristocrats was forming around him. In December 1409 he precipitated a crisis by complaining that the treasurer, Sir John Tiptoft, and the chancellor, Archbishop Arundel, had failed to honour an agreement to increase expenditure on Wales, and he forced their resignations. Tiptoft stood down on 11 December and Arundel on the 21st. The archbishop had been an unwilling head of the administration and had originally agreed to serve for one year only. He may well have had enough of the prince.

The new crisis extended for six weeks, over and beyond Christmas. The king resisted the ministerial changes forced upon him by his son and his supporters. Although a new treasurer, Henry Lord Scropeof Masham, was appointed on 6 January, it was another three weeks before a new chancellor could be found. It is likely that the king preferred to appoint a man not bound to the Prince of Wales, and that he was encouraged in this by Archbishop Arundel and Prince Thomas. For six weeks the court was the focus of intrigue as the two factions jockeyed for pre-eminence. In the end, despite his reservations, the king gave in to Prince Henry.

Parliament, which had been summoned for October 1409, was postponed until 27 January 1410. It was essential that a new chancellor be appointed for its opening. Eventually, on 31 January, the prince's man, Sir Thomas Beaufort, was sworn in. Perhaps it was to have been his brother Henry, Bishop of Winchester, but the strongly anti-clerical mood of the MPs when they assembled caused a late change of plan. The Speaker was Sir Thomas Chaucer, a Beaufort man, who had served in this role before. It was clear that from now on parliament would be conducted in the prince's interest. Through the new chancellor, he audaciously proposed that the Commons vote permanent peacetime taxation in return for a promise of good government until the end of the king's reign; in reply they proposed the partial disendowment of the Church to provide such support for the Crown.

Deadlock ensued and parliament was prorogued for Easter. When it reconvened in April the horse trading began once more. Henry secured half-subsidies for three years from 8 May; in return the administration had to concede renewal of the articles of government that had been agreed in 1406 in conjunction with parliament's continuing right to approve membership of the council.

Whether Prince Henry, who had been party to these original terms, was still happy to be bound by them or wished to be rid of such restraint, we do not know. But he accepted them. The council, as nominated, was predominantly made up of the prince's men. Parliament was dissolved on 9 May.

Government in the king's name was now effectively in the prince's hands. A budget was set in June. Priority in expenditure was given to reinforcing and revictualling Calais, to the command of which the prince had succeeded following the untimely death of the Earl of Somerset in March. At the same time the highly partisan council refused to settle Prince Thomas' debts unless he returned to Ireland. He chose to remain at court. Thomas' financial problems were solved in August when he married the heiress Margaret Holland, widow of the late Earl of Somerset. Prince Thomas was thus endowed at no cost to the Crown. Prince Henry was placed in a dilemma, for he could hardly object to an arrangement that that gave his brother an income befitting his dignity, yet it was one that could only strengthen his position at court. It seemed only a matter of time before the rivalry between the two brothers broke into open conflict.

The occasion, when it came, was a dispute over foreign policy. France was ruled by the mentally fragile Charles VI, who was frequently incapacitated. Civil war had been intermittent since the assassination in 1407 of the Duke of Orleans by his rival the Duke of Burgundy, known as John the Fearless. The English saw an opportunity to profit from French division. Prince Henry's party favoured a Burgundian alliance. But in September 1411 his father, who seems to have enjoyed a new lease of life, vetoed the initiative. In open defiance, the prince authorised a private expedition under the Earl of Arundel to help Burgundy secure Paris. A parliament, called in November to endorse this campaign, in the event witnessed the fall of the ministry. The king was fit enough to declare in person that he would tolerate no more 'novelties'. He thanked the council for its service and dismissed it. A new ministry was formed, with Archbishop Arundel returning as chancellor and Scrope being replaced as treasurer.

What the reassertive king meant by 'novelties' is not clear. He could have been referring to the manner in which the kingdom had been ruled in his name; or perhaps word had reached him that the recalcitrant prince was planning to force his abdication. Chroniclers later remarked that the younger Henry had (at some unspecified moment) had this in mind. Bishop Beaufort denied before parliament in 1426 that there was any truth in the rumour. Given the growing conflict between father and son after 1406, however, and the obvious impatience of the younger Henry to grasp the Crown, one can imagine that many observers thought there was something in it.

The change of ministry was followed by a change of strategy in France. An alliance was formed with the Armagnacs, as the Orleanist faction became known after its leadership was taken up by the forceful Bernard, Count of Armagnac, father-in-law of the new Duke of Orleans.

In exchange for military support, the count promised to concede the terms of the Treaty of Brétigny, by which an enlarged Aquitaine, Poitou and Ponthieu had been ceded to Edward III in full sovereignty. Prince Thomas himself was commissioned to lead a powerful army to France. Prince Henry was naturally affronted: he had been Duke of Aquitaine since 1399. On 17 June 1412 he published a manifesto confirming that he was raising a private force to join the expedition and that his intentions in so doing had been maliciously interpreted as rebellion by 'sons of iniquity', evil-minded persons close to the king, who sought to upset the ordered succession to the throne – he clearly had Prince Thomas in mind. Henry then marched on London, where he demanded an audience with the king. This, after a fortnight of uneasy confrontation, he was eventually granted, and a reconciliation was effected. Yet, a mere two months later, he again descended on the capital in strength, this time to demand the retraction of accusations – put out, he claimed, by his brother's men – that he had embezzled the wages of the Calais garrison. Henry's willingness to threaten force came close to treason.

Prince Henry had shown himself to be a man with an exalted view of his own importance and ability, exasperated by the restrictions placed on him as a mere subject. His behaviour and attitude incensed many who were close to the throne. The king may well have played one son off against the other so as to maintain his authority, and was perhaps not above suggesting that the succession might be amended. Prince Henry, for his part, believed that he as eldest son had the sole right to govern the kingdom if his father was incapable of doing so. Over five years he had become frustrated by the limitations placed upon him. He was impatient for power.

As it was, he had to accept the king's will. Prince Thomas, now Duke of Clarence, sailed to France on 9 August independently of his overbearing brother. He landed at Cherbourg, only to discover that the rival French princes had already made peace. Undaunted, he marched his troops through the land, looting and ransacking the countryside in a manner that brought to mind the glories of his grandfather's day. Handsomely paid off by the French, he then withdrew to Bordeaux for the winter. He was there when news reached him that his father was mortally ill. On 20 March the end came. Prince Henry was on hand to take the throne he so ardently desired.

3

'Presume not that I am the thing I was': The New King, 1413–14[4]

Henry V succeeded to the throne on 21 March 1413. He was crowned in Westminster Abbey on 9 April. No one could have been sure what manner of monarch he would make. His previous record was not entirely reassuring. Hardened in war, he was, as his first biographer wrote, 'young in years, but old in experience'.[5] He was also one of only a handful of royal heirs in English history who have been prominent in politics and government during the previous reign. This was a mixed blessing. Henry of Monmouth knew what it was like to be a subject; he was familiar with opposition, but would he be a vindictive, vengeful ruler, keen to settle old scores?

Towards the end of the reign, Thomas Walsingham commented that, as soon as he became king, Henry suddenly changed into another man: 'his care now was for self restraint and goodness and gravity and there was no kind of virtue which he put on one side and did not desire to practise himself.'[6] From this grew the legend of Prince Hal's transformation from dissolute youth to great monarch. The tale grew in the telling. An early continuation of the most widely read English chronicle describes how, as Prince of Wales, Henry 'intended [tended] greatly to riot and drew to wild company', but on becoming king 'dismissed from his household all the companions of his misspent youth bar three who had disapproved of his behaviour'.[7]

Another mid-fifteenth century chronicler, known as 'the pseudo Elmham', took this further. Prince Hal, he wrote, had been a 'diligent follower of idle practices', fervently following 'the service of Venus as well as Mars', who 'found leisure for the excesses of untamed youth'.[8] Yet another told of how, for sport, this Hooray Henry, would hold up and rob his own financial officers as they were bringing their revenues to his coffers. After 1485 the story was elaborated into the tale made familiar by Shakespeare, of the carouser, nocturnal law-breaker and keeper of low company. There is no contemporaneous evidence to support this. And, while we should not suppose that he lived chastely before he was crowned, there were (unlike his three brothers) no acknowledged illegitimate children to reveal that he had sown his wild oats.

The myth of the riotous youth drew on conventional notions of the ages of man: childhood, youth and adolescence, through which one passed before reaching full maturity as an adult. The character of Falstaff, Hal's roistering drinking companion, introduced by Shakespeare, was drawn from the real life figure of Sir John Oldcastle, a long-standing companion in arms, but also an open Lollard heretic. On becoming king, Henry did indeed distance himself and Oldcastle was banished. (Thomas Hoccleve later condemned Oldcastle for failing, like Falstaff, to be a manly knight.) Thomas Walsingham was fully aware of Henry's earlier association with Oldcastle. He almost certainly also had in mind Hal's conflict with his father and his damaging factionalism as Prince of Wales. In these ways Hal had indeed been unruly and ungoverned.

At the heart of the legend lies the prince's transformation: the moment he became king; the moment he banished 'Plump Jack' and in so doing 'banished all the world'. Rejecting the life of a mere man, he took on the persona of the model monarch and the aura of an icon. As Henry of Monmouth he had been a disruptive politician and a rebellious subject. As King Henry V of England he fashioned himself according to the precepts of the standard advice books for monarchs, known as *Mirrors for Princes*. We know that in 1410–11 Thomas Hoccleve had dedicated his work, *The Regement of Princes* (a version of *The Mirror*) to the king-in-waiting. Henry may have commissioned it or Hoccleve, a civil servant, may have offered it in the hope of further patronage. Henry presented himself to his new subjects in its terms: as the fount of justice, the protector of the Church and defender of the realm, ruling prudently within his means and listening to wise counsel. He set out to live by the highest chivalric and religious ideals. The persona he adopted when he assumed the Crown was chaste, sober, pious and dutiful. It is what he would become not what he had once been that was significant.

Notwithstanding later mythology, Henry called first upon those who had been his allies and supporters in the factional politics of the recent past. He made the urbane and wily Henry Beaufort, Bishop of Winchester, his chancellor and Thomas Fitzalan, Earl of Arundel, his treasurer – both men who had been close to him for many years. Others, including the stalwart Richard Beauchamp, Earl of Warwick, Henry Lord Scrope of Masham, the austere Henry Chichele, Bishop of St David's, and, after his return from service in Aquitaine, Sir Thomas Beaufort, Earl of Dorset, formed the core of his council.

But equally important was reconciliation with Archbishop Arundel and his brother Thomas, Duke of Clarence. Arundel remained a councillor, but died within a year, to be succeeded by Chichele. Some had feared that Clarence would dispute the Prince of Wales' right to the throne, and it was not until early 1414 that he made his peace with the new king. But thereafter he served Henry loyally until his death in 1421, a mere year before the passing of his elder brother.

Henry had two other brothers. John, two years younger, a dependable and dedicated servant to the family cause, had acted as lieutenant in the north of England since 1406. Humphrey, but one year younger than John, had played little part in public affairs during his father's reign, even though he was 23 when his father died. He was devoted to his eldest brother. All three brothers came to play crucial military and political roles as Henry's deputies without one breath of dissent. This band of brothers made a formidable team.

Henry was keenly alert to the need for continuity in the Lancastrian establishment. His reconfigured royal household contained few surprises. The ranks of the king's knights and esquires, the men who formed his inner circle domestically, politically and militarily, were nicely balanced between those who had served him as prince and those that had served his father. Past loyalty and military experience seem to have been set at a premium. Sir John Oldcastle was one of only a few who found themselves out in the cold. As steward, Henry appointed Sir Thomas Erpingham, one of his father's oldest companions, and the most respected and trusted of his servants. As chamberlain, perhaps surprisingly, he appointed Henry, Lord FitzHugh – another of his father's generation. FitzHugh had neither been involved at court nor served the prince directly, but as a soldier, crusader and model of Christian chivalry, he was an ideal choice to set the sober tone demanded of the new king's household.

FitzHugh's promotion is particularly telling, for it gives a clue to the almost monastic character of the new court. The new chamberlain was a promoter of the Brigettines, an austere order of nuns and priests founded by St Bridget of Sweden some forty years earlier. Soon after he became king, Henry set about the establishment of a religious complex surrounding his manor house at Sheen on the Thames (renamed Richmond by Henry VII). It was to be rebuilt and expanded into a royal palace. There was to be a Carthusian monastery next to the palace, in the old deer park, and a Brigettine house on the opposite bank of the river at Isleworth, to be called Syon, with a Celestine establishment – another order of hermits not unlike the Carthusians – next to it. The plan for the Celestine house was later abandoned, but on 22 February 1415 the foundation stone was laid for Syon and on 1 April the royal charter for the Charterhouse was issued. Though not fully established by the end of the king's life, the resulting complex in many ways foreshadowed (on a more modest scale) the Escorial created by Philip II of Spain 150 years later.

The new king could not be entirely confident of his position on the throne. Old divisions remained, stemming from the usurpation of Richard II in 1399. There were still many enemies unreconciled to the house of Lancaster. Rumours even resurfaced that Richard II was alive and well and hiding in Scotland. One of Henry's first decisions was to arrange an honourable and public reburial of his predecessor in Westminster Abbey. Early accounts stressed that the translation from King's Langley to the tomb the king had specially commissioned stemmed from the 'great and tender love' Henry had borne for Richard.[9] It is more likely to have been an act of atonement with hard-headed political intent, to link himself with the deposed monarch and to distance himself from his father. It also opened the way for the restoration of the heirs of those who had rebelled in Richard's name a decade or so earlier. But they had to work their passages. John Mowbray was reinstated as Earl Marshal and John Holland was restored to the Earldom of Huntingdon. Ralph Percy had to wait until 1416 to be restored to his grandfather's title of Earl of Northumberland and it was not until 1421 that Thomas

Montagu, Earl of Salisbury, secured the restoration of his father's estates.

The most serious challenge to Henry's authority came not from his dynasty's enemies but from within his own ranks. In a series of interviews in the summer of 1413 Henry sought to persuade Oldcastle to abandon his heretical beliefs. But his old friend refused to recant. He was handed over to Archbishop Arundel for trial, condemned on 25 September and returned to the Crown for burning. Henry delayed execution for forty days. On 19 October the prisoner escaped from the Tower and holed out in Clerkenwell. Later it was alleged that he sent some of his dedicated followers, disguised as mummers, to kidnap Henry and his brothers during Twelfth Night celebrations at Eltham. On 7 January, several suspects were rounded up, but again Oldcastle escaped. Three days later, other supporters coming up to London were set upon. Sixty-nine were arrested and, within a few days, thirty-eight of them were summarily tried and executed for treason, the bodies of seven being additionally burned as heretics. Commissions were immediately announced to unearth treason and heresy in London, Bristol and twenty counties throughout the land.

Henry seized on this episode to crack down on the heresy known as Lollardy. It had been a problem in England for over forty years. Henry may even have shown sympathy himself with such views as a younger man. In 1410, however, he had publicly demonstrated his orthodoxy by a dramatic intervention in the burning of one condemned heretic, John Badby, seeking unsuccessfully to persuade him to recant even as he was tied to the stake. Was he seeking at the same time to reassure those who doubted his orthodoxy? It is quite possible that the king greatly exaggerated the threat in 1413 so as to create the pretext for what was essentially a pre-emptive strike against dissidents. We have only the word of the Crown that an uprising was planned. In the aftermath a considerable number of known Lollards were arrested, often without charge or trial. Those believed to be leaders were executed, the rest held in custody for months and even years. Oldcastle remained at large and was not captured until 1417.

The Oldcastle 'uprising' presented Henry with an ideal opportunity to show that he would tolerate neither religious dissent nor street demonstration within his kingdom. He also made public show of his determination to enforce the law on other prominent figures. At the beginning of his reign a feud erupted in Shropshire between his new treasurer, the Earl of Arundel, and another of his companions in arms in Wales, John Talbot, Lord Furnival. Talbot was arrested, imprisoned in the Tower (not long after Oldcastle's escape) and, in February 1414, posted to Ireland as the king's lieutenant. Arundel escaped without punishment, but his men, along with Talbot's, were indicted before the King's Bench.

Henry had promised his first parliament, which met at Westminster in May 1413, that if he were granted the wherewithal, he would restore 'bone governance', manage his household economically and enforce public order. The House of Commons, which contained many royal friends, voted him a whole lay subsidy (the standard tax of one-fifteenth of the moveable wealth of country people, one-tenth of townsfolk) and the revenue from customs for four years. He in turn cut expenditure on Crown annuities.

In his second parliament, which met at Leicester at the end of April 1414, Henry reinforced his drive on law and order. But first he honoured his family. Thomas, Duke of Clarence, was restored to favour, John was created Duke of Bedford and Humphrey was made Duke of Gloucester. All creations were for life only. Bedford and Gloucester did not marry during Henry's lifetime, perhaps because the king did not wish it. His cousin, Edward, Duke of York, whom the king had defended in 1407, was formally cleared of any taints arising from the early years of Henry IV's reign; and his brother Richard was created Earl of Cambridge. A Statute of Lollards extended the power of the state to persecute heretics; a Statute of Riots enhanced the summary powers of justices of the peace and sheriffs. More important was the dispatch of the King's Bench to the Midlands in the summer to administer justice in several counties. This resulted in nearly 2,000 indictments, all overseen by the king in person from his headquarters in the abbey at Burton on Trent.

Thus Henry V's reign opened, with an impressive show of intent to rule firmly, to heal old wounds, to manage royal finances prudently and to enforce the law impartially, even upon those close to the king. He sought to reassure his subjects that the old days of dissension were over. But the king's main purpose was to create unity at home so that he could make war abroad. In the summer of 1414 Henry V decided that the time was ripe to announce his plan to launch an invasion of France.

4

'Now thrive the armourers': Preparation for War, 1414–15[10]

The Hundred Years war between France and England had begun in 1337. At its heart lay the claim to the throne of France put forward by Edward III. Edward had waged war, with spectacular successes won at Crécy (1346) and at Poitiers (1356) by his eldest son the Black Prince. In 1360, without surrendering his claim, he had settled by the Treaty of Brétigny for substantial territorial concessions. But in 1369, war had been reignited and over the following fifteen years a revived France had recovered most of its lost land. There had been truces, but no resolution of the underlying dispute. Towards the end of Henry IV's reign, as we have seen, the English were able to take limited advantage of French internal divisions.

Henry V had probably always intended to revive the claim to the French throne and launch a major renewal of the war as soon as he became king. He not only sought his royal birthright; he calculated that successful war abroad would reinforce harmony at home. Almost immediately after his coronation he began to re-arm. Cannon were being manufactured and stockpiled by the end of 1413. (Henry knew the value of artillery, having used heavy guns to good effect in his sieges of Aberystwyth.) Gunpowder and cannonballs followed, as did the general build-up of supplies of armour and weapons, especially thousands of bows, arrows and bowstrings. As he was equipping himself for war, he entered into negotiations with France for a 'peaceful' settlement of his 'just claims'. He maintained in all his declarations and proclamations, both for the court of Christendom and for opinion at home, that he was seeking only the settlement of his rightful demand for the recovery of his inheritance in France. Through such a just war, he added with a rhetorical flourish, he would bring a long-lasting peace.

There was no immediate change to the tempo of foreign affairs in the first months of Henry's reign. Until the autumn, when a truce with France was agreed, the two countries were technically at war. Thomas Beaufort, Earl of Dorset, who had been left in command of Aquitaine by the Duke of Clarence, raided northwards in the summer. France was a country holding several quasi-independent duchies and earldoms. Most notable among these were Brittany to the west and Burgundy to the east, whose dukes cut independent figures on the international stage. The power of Burgundy was enhanced by the possession of Flanders, Brabant and neighbouring counties and lordships in what are now the Benelux countries. But there were other powerful territorial blocs too, ruled by the Dukes of Orleans and Berry, the Counts of Anjou and Armagnac, as well as the Duchy of Aquitaine held by the kings of England. Only in the central northern region, the île de France and the Loire valley did the Crown hold direct sway. This was the France with which Henry negotiated.

First he renewed existing truces not only with Scotland and Aragon, but also with the French princes of Brittany and Burgundy. Events allowed Henry to begin to put diplomatic pressure on France. The fragile truce between the Burgundians and Armagnacs broke down shortly after he was crowned. The Duke of Burgundy fled Paris and civil war was renewed. Henry's ambassadors negotiated with both parties, first seeking a marriage alliance either with Charles VI's daughter, Catherine, or Burgundy's daughter, another Catherine. As civil war intensified in France, so Henry's ambitions swelled. Terms for an offensive alliance were discussed with a Burgundian delegation in April 1414, and their duke agreed to recognise the English claim to full sovereignty in Aquitaine.

Playing one against the other, the king sent a powerful embassy to Paris in July 1414. Under the pretence of seeking a general settlement of all issues and a perpetual peace between the two kingdoms, the embassy was instructed to make an outrageous demand: the complete restoration of all the lands in France ever held by the kings of England since 1066 as part of the price of the marriage to Catherine of Valois. No negotiations with the French since 1360 had gone beyond demanding the full implementation of the terms of the Treaty of Brétigny. To go back to 1205 and the loss of Normandy was novel to say the least. Negotiations were cut short, however, by yet another truce between the Armagnacs and the hard-pressed Burgundians.

It is almost certain that by this time Henry's intention to invade France, though not officially declared, was known to all parties. He now had to adjust his diplomatic strategy. The first step was to go public. Another parliament was summoned. The chancellor declared at its opening, on 19 November, that the king would 'strive for the recovery of the inheritance and right of his crown outside the realm which has for a long time been withheld and wrongfully kept'.[11] To enable him to 'strive for justice', the Commons were asked to vote a double lay subsidy. They approved the tax, but insisted upon a further round of negotiation.

Ambassadors returned to France in February 1415. Given a new unity in France and the need to appear to be seeking a peaceful solution, Henry's demands were less brazen. But they were still designed to be unacceptable. The French, however, were increasingly confident that they could take him on. It was possibly at this time that the Dauphin Louis, very much the driving force at court, sent an insulting message suggesting that the king would be better advised to stay at home and play tennis rather than risk war – immortalised by Shakespeare as a gift of tennis balls. The negotiations duly failed.

By April 1415 both countries were on a war footing. Henry had been preparing for almost two years; the French, united again, had been anticipating an invasion since the summer of the 1414. Henry called a council of his peers to Westminster at which he commissioned them to recruit for a nine-month campaign. He led by example, calling out all his own knights and esquires with their men and avowing his intention to take his whole household with him, including his chamber and the staff of the royal chapel. He began to assemble an armada of ships to transport this army, and he started to raise loans, underwritten by promises of future taxation and pledges of royal jewels and plate. Measures were taken to reinforce the border with Scotland and to guard against a revival of the Welsh rebellion. His brothers, Clarence and Gloucester, were to accompany him overseas, while the ever-dependable Bedford was to be installed as Keeper of the Realm in his absence, with a handful of chosen peers and councillors to support him.

There were feverish last-minute negotiations: by the English to detach Burgundy and Brittany; and by the French to delay the invasion so as to complete their own preparations. To this end they sent envoys to England. The king met them at Winchester early in July. He debated with them himself, the only recorded occasion in which he negotiated personally, and was reported to have lost his temper with their time wasting. D-day was set for 1 August. Nothing was to stop him.

The French had one last ploy: to seek to exploit divisions and resentments in England and to disrupt the king's plans at the eleventh hour. One French double agent later reported that there was much disquiet at the highest levels in England about the wisdom of the campaign, that some believed a good peace could have been achieved by a marriage alliance and that there was talk of replacing the king. For all his confidence and bravura, Henry V still looked over his shoulder to the flaw in his title to the throne and the lingering threats he faced as a result of the taint of usurpation. One powerful factor in his desire to go to war was to seek God's judgement and removal of this taint: to unite his kingdom behind him once and for all through victory on the field of battle.

Sure enough, there was a plot to stop the war. On 31 July, Edmund Mortimer, Earl of March, in many eyes the true heir to Richard II, came before the king at Porchester Castle to confess his part in treasonable discussion. He informed the king that Richard, Earl of Cambridge, Sir Thomas Grey of Heaton, Northumberland, and Henry Scrope, Lord Masham, planned to seize him, raise Wales in Mortimer's name and call out the far north in the name of the exiled but not yet restored Earl of Northumberland. He, March, was to be put on the throne.

This was the so-called Southampton Plot. Edmund Mortimer had been in the king's household, under careful watch for several years. Henry had recently fined him heavily for marrying without his consent. Cambridge, younger brother of the highly favoured Duke of York, was disgruntled because he had not received an endowment from the king worthy of his newly awarded title. Scrope is the most puzzling conspirator. He had been a close companion of the king for many years, treasurer in 1409–10, still high in favour and a member of the embassies sent to France in 1414 and 1415. He subsequently claimed to have engaged with the plotters on the king's behalf, so as to dissuade them, himself intending no treason.

March was pardoned. The other three were arrested, tried at Southampton on 2 August and executed three days later. The confessions of both March and Scrope, subsequently published, indicate that it was a plot in its early stages – barely even that – to be carried out in the king's absence. Only later was it put out that they had planned to kill Henry. It has been suggested that the king seized the opportunity of March's tip off to secure confessions in what amounted to a show trial, designed to make it appear both more serious and at the same time more futile than it was. Here was an opportunity to demonstrate that he would brook no opposition and to underline the fate awaiting any, even one of his closest servants, who dared question his policy and actions. The victims were executed. Two heads were sent to be displayed over city gates: Scrope at York and Grey at Newcastle-upon-Tyne. The Earl of Cambridge did not suffer the same indignity; he was buried intact at Southampton. Scrope was guilty only of misprision, failure to report treason. Not only was his treatment mean, unforgiving and vindictive (his last will was not acknowledged), but the whole process was conducted without due process. Legality was only conferred retrospectively by parliament in November. Something of the king's private self was revealed in all this.

The departure of the royal expedition was delayed over a week by the Southampton Plot. When the armada eventually set sail on the afternoon of 11 August, it transported an army of at least 11,000 combatants, most in mixed companies of men-at-arms and archers. Archers, including some in independent battalions, alone numbered

9,000. Then there was the artillery train – gunners and their guns, together with miners, blacksmiths, armourers, carpenters and stonemasons. In addition came the non-combatants – chaplains, pages and grooms attached to each unit – taking the total number of personnel towards 15,000. The host was mounted, many taking several horses: there were possibly 30,000 in all. In total, 1,500 ships were needed to transport the assembled mass. No larger force had sailed to France since 1346. All were required to bring victuals for three months. Henry had learnt the lessons of Wales. He had put together a fully paid, provisioned and equipped army ready for all eventualities.

Until the expedition set sail few knew its destination. One widely mentioned option was Bordeaux, where safe landing would be certain and a campaign could strike deep into the heart of France. But communications were long and the loyalty of the Gascons fickle. Normandy was nearer and offered the prospect of securing another base in northern France from which to launch further campaigns. So Normandy it was: the target Harfleur, a recently fortified naval base from which the English could also protect shipping in the Channel. After a calm crossing, the fleet sailed into the mouth of the Seine on 13 August and anchored just below the town. The war that was to preoccupy the king for the rest of his reign had begun.

5

'The game's afoot': Harfleur and Agincourt, 1415[12]

It took two days to disembark. King Henry came ashore on the 14th, the vigil of the Assumption of the Blessed Virgin Mary. In full view of all, he dropped to his knees, praying for God to give him justice. The landing was unopposed. By 17 August Harfleur was besieged. The king set up camp to the west, on high ground. Clarence was to the east. A code of military discipline was issued, stressing obedience to orders, respect for clergy and women, and clarifying the procedures for the treatment of prisoners. The king, it was later reported, toured the lines every night, praising those who had performed well, reprimanding those who had not. He set up a temporary royal chapel in which his chaplains sang Mass daily. He was determined to keep God on his side.

Harfleur had some thousand defenders. It was well protected by large walls and, to afford further defence, the townsmen had flooded the nearby River Lézarde, which flowed to the west and south before entering the Seine. The garrison refused to surrender. So it was subjected to relentless bombardment.

The siege lasted five weeks. It coincided with a heat wave. The English army lived in cramped, insanitary quarters, which were soon awash with rotting waste, decaying bodies and excrement. The flooded defences of the town became a stinking bog. Shigella dysentery broke out in both camps, especially the king's, close to the swamp. Among the deaths on the English side were the Bishop of Norwich and Earl of Suffolk. Many others were severely incapacitated. The failure of a French attempt to break the siege by river and a limited English success in seizing one of the barbicans finally led the garrison to negotiate. Terms were agreed for surrender on 22 September if no French army had appeared by then. Hostages were handed over to the king: they were met under the city walls by a procession of the whole royal chapel in their finest copes, singing anthems of praise and thanksgiving. On the appointed day the keys were solemnly handed over to Henry sitting in majesty in his pavilion. The victor was magnanimous, although he subsequently expelled all citizens who refused to give their allegiance. The town was to be turned into a second Calais and immigrants were encouraged from England to populate it for the Crown.

It had taken longer than expected to reduce Harfleur. The cost had been high and supplies were dwindling. Henry, who had recruited an army for nine months in the field, had probably intended to move on to Rouen by this time, and then Paris. He was forced to change his plan. He knew that the dauphin had a large army east of Rouen, so he decided to march to Calais. On 26 September he challenged the dauphin to personal combat to settle their dispute. Not surprisingly, Louis did not even respond. Henry then repatriated all the sick and wounded – including the Earl of Arundel, who died shortly after arriving home, and his own brother, Thomas, who recovered. Having placed a garrison of 1,200 men with the artillery in Harfleur under the Earl of Dorset, he struck camp on 8 October. His total force now probably numbered no more than 9,000, which was considerably smaller than the original army – but still sizeable.

It is not certain whether Henry intended to force battle en route. The chaplain in his company, who wrote the *Gesta Henrici Quinti* with hindsight, stated that his liege had wished for battle so that the few could triumph over the many. Henry would certainly have been prepared for this eventuality, for the dauphin's army lay between him and his destination. He may equally have hoped to have reached Calais without confrontation, but left it to God to decide.

The English army swung through Arques, bypassing Eu, and made for the ford over the Somme at Blanchetague. But the French reached there first. Rather than risk an engagement, Henry turned his troops inland and upstream, looking for another crossing point. All the time the enemy shadowed them along the far bank. Having optimistically planned for an eight-day march to Calais, supplies soon began to run short. The army resorted to living off the land. The king struggled to maintain discipline. Public example was made of one soldier who stole a pyx (a jewelled box for the consecrated sacrament) from a church – an incident immortalised by Shakespeare in Bardolph's fate. On 19 October, they found an unguarded ford and were fortunate to make an unopposed crossing. The next day, as they marched north again, Henry accepted a formal challenge to battle on 24 October. Marching as rapidly as he could, he found the French drawn up beyond the village of Maisoncelle. By the time they reached the battlefield, the English were hungry and exhausted.

Overnight it poured with rain. At first light on St Crispin's and St Crispinian's day, the English took up defensive positions to await the French onslaught. They were arranged in the customary three battles, with archers deployed in between and to the flanks. The king, in command of the centre, dressed conspicuously, a crown on his helm to make sure that he was visible to the enemy. Later accounts and mythology make out that the English were outnumbered by five to one or more. Recent, closer analysis of the contemporaneous descriptions from both sides suggests that this was not the case. Against the 9,000 English combatants, the French fielded at least 12,000 and may be up to 15,000 (including a far greater number of non-combatants). The sense of greater disparity in the numbers probably arose from the fact that the French army was composed predominantly of fully armoured and mounted men-at-arms, amounting to about three-quarters of their number. On the English side the ratio was reversed, with archers outnumbering men-at-arms by three to one. In terms of elite troops, the English were indeed heavily outnumbered. Moreover, French reinforcements were still arriving on the morning of the 25th, and it was probably for this reason that they delayed attacking for several hours.

Battle began when Henry V ordered his men to move forward, in formation, either to take up new positions within firing range of the French or, more likely, to appear to be advancing to provoke an attack before dropping back. Moving the whole line was a dangerous manoeuvre for it entailed the archers wading through mud, either carrying their protective stakes with them or leaving them behind. But the manoeuvre achieved its objective of provoking the French vanguard (larger, in fact, than the main guard) to attack. They had not chosen their ground wisely. Their army was cramped between two woods, the village of Agincourt being on their right. As they advanced in two huge battle lines, one behind the other, they were funnelled closer together and became easier targets for the hail of English arrows. Moreover, the ploughed field across which they and their horses attempted to charge was soon turned into a mud bath.

As it approached, the advancing French phalanx split into three columns, throwing themselves at each of the English battle lines. The archers maintained a constant hail of shot, from the front and into their flanks, at ten or more a minute, until their arrows were all used. Bolts like bullets could pierce armour at short range. The effect was similar to that of machine-gun fire five centuries later. Heavily armoured bodies piled on top of one another. Only a few made it through to Henry's lines. Most successful was the column attacking the English right. The Duke of York, in command of that section, was killed along with several other notables before the assault was thrown back. The central column eventually reached the king, who fought long and hard, at one moment standing over and saving his youngest brother Humphrey who had fallen.

The battle became a massacre as the French finally lost impetus, the English advanced and the archers encircled their enemy in hand-to-hand fighting. Seeing the disaster unfolding before them, the French main guard held back. Late in the engagement a squadron of cavalry outflanked the English line and destroyed the baggage train. There was no question of pursuit. The English sorted the dead from the living in the piles of bodies before them, collected prisoners and moved them to the rear. At this moment, a report came to the king that the main guard was preparing to attack. Without seeking confirmation, he instantly ordered the killing of prisoners. In fact, no such second attack occurred; the main guard was withdrawing from the field.

English casualties were relatively low, the only noble deaths being the Duke of York and the Earl of Suffolk (he had been earl for but one month since succeeding his father who had died of dysentery on the campaign). A few hundred English foot soldiers were killed. Many more French died: 4,000 is the lowest estimate. Even allowing for the cold-blooded killing of some prisoners, at least 300 'men of name' survived and possibly as many as a thousand, all told, came back to England to be ransomed. The French defeat was not down to overconfidence so much as poor leadership and tactics: battle plans had been changed at the last minute and the inexperienced 21-year old Duke of Orleans had put himself in command of the vanguard. Most of the other noblemen followed him so as not to be outdone in a show of courage, leaving no one of stature and tactical acumen to command the main guard.

Henry had overthrown the whole might of France, including Armagnacs and Burgundians united in the face of their old enemy. Neither the Dukes of Burgundy nor Brittany had fought, but their brothers had led contingents. Burgundy's brother had been killed and Brittany's taken prisoner (like Orleans, another survivor not murdered on the field). This was indeed a famous victory, if not quite so much against the odds as later mythology has made it. It was, however, marred by the massacre of the prisoners, for which many have endeavoured to exculpate Henry, either in terms of the strict laws of war or of military necessity.

Agincourt was a decisive battle. It was the high point of the domination of the longbow in battlefield tactics. It established Henry V's chivalric and martial fame, and made him a general feared and respected by his enemies. The French were, for the rest of his life, exceedingly wary of facing the English in open, formal battle. The battle's lasting fame, greater than the comparable victory at Crécy, is probably because Henry V assiduously associated it with national endeavour and national glory, for 'Harry, England and St George'. A miraculous victory snatched from the jaws of defeat, celebrated in popular song and verse, especially *The Agincourt Carol*, and commemorated every year with an anniversary service of thanksgiving at Westminster Abbey, the Battle of Agincourt rapidly became and has remained a symbol of English national pride.

The road to Calais was now open. There was no time for Christian burial of the dead, English or French. The English were cremated, apart from those lords whose bodies were boiled down for the return home. The French, stripped for loot, were left where they lay. Henry's army arrived in Calais on 29 October. It took several days for the weary troops to cross the Channel. The king himself did not sail until mid-November and suffered a very rough crossing. From Dover he made stately progress, stopping at Canterbury to give thanks for his victory, and arriving on Blackheath a week later, where he was formally welcomed by a delegation from the city of London. His triumphal entry into the capital on 23 November along the accustomed route for such victory parades was carefully orchestrated according to his advance instructions. The images of a giant and of St George were placed on London Bridge. The city conduits flowed with wine. Church bells rang out and beacons were lit. The dominant theme was 'Praise to God', while the king himself rode with just a few companions, modestly and simply attired. His noble French prisoners followed behind, though not in chains as they would have in a Roman triumph.

A parliament had been called and met (4–17 November) in his absence. A grateful House of Commons voted the king all of the revenue from customs for the rest of his life, together with another round of additional subsidies. All doubts about Henry's right to rule had been obliterated in the muddy field of Agincourt.

6

'Once more into the breach': The Conquest of Normandy, 1416–19[13]

The walls of France had been breached. Henry planned to renew and intensify the assault as soon as he could. There are indications that he may even have been tempted to continue campaigning in France until November. But his troops were exhausted and supplies had run out, so he wisely returned home to recruit a new army. In the event he did not cross the Channel again until 1417.

The immediate military need was to supply Harfleur and complete the rebuilding of its defences. Once they had overcome the shock of Agincourt, the French were determined to recover the town. The 18-year-old Dauphin Louis, who had emerged as an independent figure capable of re-establishing royal authority, died in December 1415. The Count of Armagnac tightened his control of royal government in France as a result. As captain general of the army, he moved troops to Normandy. By spring, Harfleur was blockaded by land and sea.

Henry had already indicated his intention to raise a new army. In January 1416 he summoned council to discuss a second expedition. The knights and esquires of his household were put on stand by. A parliament was called for 16 March. There he secured the advance payment of an instalment of tax not due until November. Aware of the serious situation in Harfleur, efforts were redirected to the raising of a navy to break the blockade. But all preparations for immediate action were set aside by the arrival in May of the King of the Romans (the formal title of the Emperor Elect) Sigismund, on a peace mission.

Sigismund had been the moving spirit behind the convening of the Council of Constance in 1414. Its aim had been to tackle heresy, reform the Church and end the Schism which had occurred in 1378, with two rival popes holding office simultaneously, one in Rome and another in Avignon. Since 1409 the number of claimants had risen to three. The council had persuaded two to abdicate, but the third, Benedict XIII, had been officially recognised by France and obdurately refused to resign. The unity of the Council of Constance was disrupted by Anglo-French rivalry. Sigismund's entreaties in France had not been well received. In contrast, his reception in England was lavish and positive. He was even elected a Knight of the Garter. Henry's aim was to secure Sigismund as an ally against France and to use the debate within the Church as a platform to promote the English cause. Sigismund wanted peace through negotiation; Henry sought peace through war.

The King of the Romans' extended stay in England meant that Henry could not take personal command of the fleet to relieve Harfleur. In his stead he appointed his brother John, Duke of Bedford, to overall naval command. On 15 August, almost exactly a year since Henry V's landing in 1415, the English fleet, with a fighting force of some 5,000 men on board, appeared in the mouth of the Seine and attacked the Franco-Castilian ships blocking Harfleur. After a seven-hour battle Bedford was victorious. Harfleur was relieved.

On the same day as this Battle of the Seine, Henry and Sigismund sealed what became known as the Treaty of Canterbury, whereby the King of the Romans pledged to support the King of the English in his just campaign in France. It was an endorsement which enhanced the legitimacy of Henry's cause immeasurably, but had little practical impact. In the event Sigismund did not provide any military aid for his new ally. By the time he left England other diplomatic initiatives had been taken. An embassy had been sent to Paris to discuss once again (and with equal prospect of success) a final peace between the two kingdoms. More importantly, envoys had been sent to Calais to pave the way for a personal meeting between King Henry and Duke John 'the Fearless' of Burgundy. Relations between the duke and the Armagnacs had once more turned sour. Crucially, the new 17-year-old Dauphin, who had been married since 1406 to Burgundy's niece, was at the time of his brother's death in the household of his mother-in-law, the sister of Duke John. With the heir to throne in his pocket, John the Fearless saw the opportunity to recover power in France, towards which end an English alliance might help.

Count William of Holland, the dauphin's father-in-law, had joined King Sigismund in London in the summer and no doubt it was then that negotiations with Henry had begun. Discussions came to a head with a meeting in Calais in October, at which Sigismund was also present.

The English objective was a triple alliance against France in which Burgundy recognised Henry's right to the throne. No public agreement was reached other than the extension of the truce, but there may have been a secret understanding that, in exchange for neutrality, Henry would do nothing to stop Burgundy's recovery of power in Paris. In the event it all came to nothing, for the dauphin, continuing his family's tradition of ill health, died in January 1417. The new dauphin, his younger brother Charles, was firmly in the Armagnac camp.

By the beginning of 1417, Henry's preparations for his second invasion of France were well under way. Yet another parliament had assembled at Westminster on 19 October 1416. Exhorted by Bishop Beaufort to 'make war so that we might have peace', the Commons voted another double subsidy. The clergy in their convocation were similarly generous. Once more indentures were sealed, troops recruited, artillery, bows and arrows collected, and a navy impressed from the ports of England. This time the army was some 10,000 strong (12,000 including non-combatants), smaller than in 1415.

Once again the invasion fleet set off from Southampton. It landed on 1 August, not in Harfleur where it was expected, but at Touques on the Normandy beaches near modern Deauville, on the other side of the Seine estuary. The English army took only a day to disembark. Striding ashore, Henry laid down a formal challenge to Charles VI to cede to him his just rights or face the consequences. He came, he reiterated, so that peace could be restored.

Henry's prime objective was to conquer and occupy Normandy. His strategy was to take lower Normandy first since it was further from Paris, then move on Rouen and upper Normandy. He was confident that no French army would oppose him. There may well have been an understanding between Henry and Burgundy, for Duke John simultaneously launched his own assault on the Armagnacs in the Seine valley, rapidly taking Pontoise and several places south and west of Paris. His aim was the seizure of the king and the new dauphin. Without this concurrent civil war in France, Henry could never have achieved his objective.

The first English target was Caen, the capital of lower Normandy. Henry's army arrived before its walls on 18 August. It was more strongly fortified than Harfleur and well garrisoned. The customary demand to surrender was rejected and a date was agreed for submission should help not arrive. After two weeks of siege, however, and having gained access to the monastery of St Etienne abutting its walls, the king ordered a general assault. While he led the attack on one side, drawing defenders to that section of the walls, Clarence scaled an undefended section and entered the city. The town was brutally sacked and pillaged. Under the law of arms, civilians who refused to surrender were at the mercy of their conqueror. Many were murdered. Others, who would not render homage, were expelled and their property confiscated.

After a few days the army moved on. The fate of Caen was a dire warning to all who dared resist Henry. Many towns were fortified and garrisoned but surrendered without a fight. Alençon, Mortain and Belleme and their counties were in English hands within weeks. The Duke of Brittany came to Alençon to reaffirm his truce; Anjou and Maine followed suit. Soon all that was left unconquered was Falaise, birthplace of William the Conqueror, an imposing fortress south of Caen. Its castle did not fall until mid-February.

Tools, weapons, provisions and, most importantly, cash to pay the troops were being regularly shipped across the Channel to Caen. In March 1418 reinforcements of 2,000 men also arrived. King Henry celebrated St George's day in Caen Castle. The conquest continued. A detachment under the Duke of Gloucester was sent to complete the subjection of western Normandy, culminating in the fall of Cherbourg, the only remaining place to offer sustained resistance, in September. To the east English control soon extended as far as the Seine.

Henry now set himself to reorganise the government and administration of the conquered lands. English captains were appointed to all the principal towns and English garrisons placed in them. Civil administration was co-ordinated through the *baillies*, the equivalent of the sheriffs of English counties. Their offices were systematically anglicised. Lordships and lands were redistributed to his henchmen and to Normans who had rendered homage. Caen and Bayeux, like Harfleur, were opened up to English settlers. This was not just a conquest – it was an occupation. Henry, as the heir to William I, had come to recapture and repossess his ancestral duchy.

On 29 May, a Burgundian party broke into Paris. Bernard, Count of Armagnac, and his principal lieutenants were hunted down and murdered. A general massacre followed. The infirm King Charles VI was 'rescued' and brought into the care of Duke John. But the 15-year-old Dauphin Charles escaped with a surviving cohort of Armagnacs and fled south to Bourges. Now finally in control of the capital and the kingdom, Burgundy took steps to oppose English progress beyond Normandy. Henry had already launched his summer offensive, moving north to secure the crossing of the Seine at Pont-de-l'Arche on 20 July. Rouen lay before him.

The siege began on 1 August, a year to the day after the landing at Touques. Rouen was more strongly defended, more substantially victualled and more formidably walled than any place Henry had yet reduced. The citizens had even razed the suburbs to the ground in preparation for battle. Henry established four camps around the walls, linked by heavily defended trenches. River access from upstream was blocked by a great chain. The captain of Caudebec, which lay between Harfleur and Rouen, undertook not to hinder English river traffic. Preparations in place, Henry's army sat down to starve the city out.

Autumn turned to winter. Occasional sallies and skirmishes relieved the tedium. As hunger intensified, the old and infirm were sent out of the city into no-man's-land, where the king callously let them die, despite the entreaties of his more soft-hearted captains. 'I put them not there,' he is reported to have declared.[14] Finally, at the beginning of January, the citizens treated to surrender; they did so on 19 January 1419.

Thomas Beaufort, now Duke of Exeter, received the surrender. The following day Henry took the submission of his subjects. He was more magnanimous to the citizens of Rouen than he had been to those of Caen. This was to be his capital as Duke of Normandy, the seat of civil and ecclesiastical government for the whole duchy, so he made sure his troops were not let loose. 'His' city was fined heavily for not recognising him, but lives were spared and property restored to all who accepted his rule. There were no expulsions. This was, in its wider significance, his greatest victory, for it sealed the conquest of Normandy, the reunification of the duchy with England and was the first milestone on the 'recovery' of his kingdom of France.

The Duke of Burgundy had made no effort to relieve Rouen. He and his army sat still at Pontoise. He likewise allowed Henry to complete the occupation of Normandy. The whole of the Pays de Caux, north and west of Rouen and Dieppe, was in English hands by the middle of March. The eastern marches as far as Vernon and Mantes surrendered by May. Only Gisors, on the far eastern border, remained to be recovered, and this was achieved in September. In two years, unopposed in the field, Henry had occupied Normandy. He was now, emphatically, Duke of Normandy as well as Aquitaine, and a major player in French affairs. The time had come to look for the peace that was the end of war.

7

'The vasty fields of France': War and Peace, 1419–22[15]

Negotiations began in earnest at the end of May 1419. Henry continued to play one party against the other. Proposals had been put to the dauphin during the winter. They had led nowhere. It was to Burgundy, who controlled the government of the realm in the name of Charles VI, that Henry now turned. He insisted that he held Normandy as its rightful duke and that the Normans were his subjects. Tight discipline was maintained accordingly, in order to avoid wanton looting – the usual recourse of an invading army. To ensure continued self-control, the troops needed to be paid and supplied regularly. No parliament had been called in 1418, so no new taxation raised. The last subsidies voted in the autumn of 1417 had been collected in February 1418 and again the following year. Henry relied heavily on these to underwrite loans. He also pledged further crown jewels. It was essential to keep his army in the field. By the summer of 1419 the strain was beginning to tell.

Negotiations for a settlement with the Duke of Burgundy and Charles VI took place at Meulan in June. Henry's demands remained the same: the restitution of all the territories ceded by the Treaty of Brétigny with the addition of Normandy in full sovereignty. In other words, he demanded the partition of France.

Burgundy would concede only Aquitaine and Normandy. Even before Henry had time to reject this suggestion, on 11 July the Duke of Burgundy pulled out of discussions and made peace with the dauphin, both agreeing not to treat with the English. The truce between Burgundy and England expired on 29 July. That night Henry sent a small party to surprise and scale the walls of an unprepared Pontoise. This daring raid, which cost little, opened the road to Paris and put Burgundy under new pressure. Further raids were carried out – to St Denis and even as far as the walls of Paris.

The Burgundians and Armagnacs had agreed in July that Duke John and the dauphin would meet personally to decide on joint action against the English. They assembled on Montereau Bridge, south-east of Paris, on 10 September. Elaborate security measures were taken, the principals and their closest advisers meeting in the middle of the bridge in a specially fenced compound. The duke knelt before the dauphin. As he arose he was struck down and killed by one or more of the dauphin's attendants. The murders of the Duke of Orleans in 1407 and Count of Armagnac the year before were thus royally avenged, but at enormous political cost. A meeting that had promised reconciliation and a united front instead drove the Burgundians back into the English camp. It was later said that Henry 'entered France through the hole in the Duke of Burgundy's skull'.

Henry was not slow to take advantage of the assassination. He immediately reopened negotiations with the new duke, Philip. Meanwhile, his representatives appeared before the *parlement* of Paris and declared fresh terms for peace: nothing short of the disinheritance of the dauphin and the adoption of Henry as heir to Charles VI. He, Henry, would restore peace to France. After careful discussion with his advisers, Philip agreed to consider the terms. There was a continuous flow of diplomatic activity over the winter as the details were finalised, including the long-mooted marriage between Henry and Charles VI's youngest daughter, Catherine, which had been at the core of all negotiations for a lasting peace since 1413. On Christmas Eve a general truce between England and France was declared.

The next step was for Charles VI formally to agree to the disinheritance of his heir and to seal a binding treaty. It took a further three months of wrangling to agree a text. At last, when all was prepared, Henry V journeyed in state to Troyes, where the French king had been residing for several months. On 21 May 1420 the treaty was sealed and Henry and Catherine were formally betrothed. They were married on 2 June with appropriate pomp and ceremony in the parish church of St John, but with relatively few in attendance and most of those English. Peace, the end of Henry's war, it was declared, had been achieved.

The Treaty of Troyes was a simple document. It focused on the marriage of Henry and Catherine as the means of uniting the houses of Lancaster and Valois, and on the consequent disinheritance of the dauphin. It set down that Henry, the new heir to the French throne, would rule as regent during the rest of Charles VI's lifetime. Henry took on responsibility for enforcing a lasting settlement of the civil war in France. It was made clear that once he became king the two realms of England and France would remain separate, with all their laws and customs unchanged: it was to be a dual monarchy not a united kingdom. The treaty was thus purely a dynastic settlement. All subjects of Charles VI were to take an oath accepting its terms.

There lay the rub. Neither the dauphin, now 18, nor his numerous supporters would take the oath. Indeed, they quickly proclaimed that the treaty was illegal, for no King of France had the power to disinherit a legally acknowledged dauphin. As well as the dauphinists, several towns and many lords also refused to swear. Henry was going to have to enforce the peace by further war if he were to destroy the future Charles VII. Campaigning with the Duke of Burgundy, he reduced Sens to obedience. Montereau was a harder nut to crack; it did not fall until 1 July, its capitulation preceded by the hanging, in full view of the walls, of eighteen prisoners as a reprisal for the murder of an English knight. Then it was Melun, which proved even more difficult and did not succumb until November. Once more prisoners were executed in reprisal. If he ever thought enforcing the treaty was going to be easy, the new regent was quickly disabused.

It was not until the winter of 1420 that Henry was free to parade his triumph. On 1 December he was accorded a joyous entry into Paris. Six days later, a specially convened, but by no means fully attended, session of the rarely assembled Estates General of France confirmed the treaty. After Christmas the royal cavalcade set off for England via Rouen, Amiens and Calais. King and queen landed at Dover on 1 February. Henry went ahead to London to co-ordinate yet another royal entry for his new bride, who was due to arrive three weeks later. The culmination of the show was her coronation at Westminster Abbey on 23 February 1421. At about this time she conceived.

Henry was soon back to other affairs of state. Parliament having been summoned for 2 May, he set off on a hurried tour of his kingdom to rally support in recruits and loans: to Bristol, the Welsh border counties, the Midlands (he spent Easter at Leicester), then north to York, with time for a brief pilgrimage to Bridlington. He was at Beverley at the end of March when he heard of the death of his brother Thomas, Duke of Clarence, his royal deputy in France, killed at Beaugé with many of his captains. Henry determined to return as soon as possible to avenge him.

First, however, the king needed to attend to parliament and complete the raising of reinforcements. The Treaty of Troyes was placed before the Commons and Lords for ratification. This formality completed, Henry's main concern was to secure another grant of taxation to underwrite the loans he had secured. The exchequer was desperately short of funds, but no tax was forthcoming. Henry reassured MPs that the two kingdoms would be ruled separately and that he had no intention of introducing French law into England. In which case, the Commons insisted, the French taxpayer should foot the bill for the enforcement of the treaty. In the end the convocation of Canterbury came to the rescue with the vote of a clerical tax.

The royal recruitment drive proved disappointing. Many of the Yorkshire gentry to whom Henry appealed to raise men were ready with quick excuses, a surprising number claiming ill health. One even argued that he was no true gentleman and thus unfit to bear arms. War weariness was clearly setting in. Nevertheless the king was able to raise an army of just over 4,000 men. And so it was back to France once more to make good the damage done at Beaugé. He sailed from Dover on 10 June, having made a new will the day before.

The Dauphin Charles had not been idle in the meantime. In 1418, a full year before the assassination of John the Fearless, he had sought foreign aid from Castile, Savoy, Lombardy and Scotland. His Scottish appeal was the most successful. Under their belligerent regent, the Duke of Albany, the Scots had already tried to open a northern front in 1417. The Auld Alliance having been revived, on 19 October 1419 a fleet arrived at La Rochelle carrying 6,000 Scots to aid the dauphin. Their presence was felt immediately. It was a combined Franco-Scottish army which had overthrown Clarence at Beaugé on 22 March 1421. In the aftermath of the battle they pressed their offensive into the southern marches of Normandy before being repulsed by the Earl of Salisbury.

In response to the Scottish intervention, Henry V summoned to his side the King of Scots, James I, who had been in English captivity since 1406. James I campaigned with him thereafter, even against fellow Scots, most notably at the siege of Meaux. Henry V's first objective in the summer of 1421 was to reassert the initiative. He first took Dreux, then marched quickly south towards Orleans where he sought to remove the dauphin in one decisive battle. The cautious Charles refused to be drawn, though the armies came close to each other near Beaugency. Instead, he slipped back behind the safety of the Loire and retired to Bourges, which he had made his base. Short of supplies, and with sickness once again threatening his army, Henry was forced to turn back to Paris. He now decided to reduce Meaux, a dauphinist outpost to the east of the capital. Beginning on 6 October, it was to be the third winter siege of his campaign, and the longest, most difficult and most costly of all. Not until the following May was Meaux completely subdued. And by then Henry's own health was beginning to fail.

Rumours had been spreading for some time that he was ill. He had driven himself relentlessly and had shared the rough conditions of his men in several sieges. Constant campaigning had taken its toll. The morale of his troops was beginning to falter too. The dauphin had not rolled over as planned; the Burgundians had been less than wholehearted in their military support; enthusiasm back home was waning; money was less readily available. At the siege of Meaux, Sir John Cornwall's son was killed by a cannonball while standing next to his father. Sir John, one of the king's longest-standing and most devoted captains, was reported to have declared that he had come to conquer Normandy, not depose the dauphin, and that he was going home. He retired soon after.

There was time for one more action: the taking of Compiègne. Thereafter the king delegated to others the subjugation of dauphinist outposts to the north and east of Paris. He withdrew to Vincennes, east of the capital, where he celebrated Whitsun with his queen, newly arrived in France escorted by the Duke of Bedford and a thousand fresh troops. She had left their 6-month-old baby son at home: Henry was never to see him.

Despite failing health – modern conjecture is that he might have caught dysentery at the siege of Meaux or suffered from toxic megaclonitis (arising from an inflamed bowel) – Henry took to the field again to lay siege to Cosny. But he could make it only as far as Corbeil. No longer able to ride, he was conveyed back to Vincennes by boat. There he began to put his affairs in order. At his bedside were his closest companions in arms: Bedford, Exeter and FitzHugh (who had been present, managing his household, from the very first day of his reign). On his deathbed Henry asked forgiveness for his sins and for the harm he had caused, especially his treatment of the heirs of Lord Scrope, and regretted that he had not been able to lead a crusade to Jerusalem. At the last, so it was to be told, he cried out against demons trying to seize his soul. He died in the early hours of 31 August 1422, his soul shriven, consummately performing in his death the role of saintly monarch he had perfected in his life. The kingdoms of England and France, we are assured by Walsingham, were united in mourning.

8

'Gentlemen in England now abed': The Home Front, 1417–22[16]

Apart from four months in 1421, Henry V was away from England for the last five years of his reign. In his absence the kingdom was governed by his brothers, the Dukes of Bedford and Gloucester, in rotation, aided by a standing council. Bedford held the office of keeper (*Custos*) until the end of 1419, when he was relieved by Gloucester, who held the position until the king's return in February 1421. Bedford resumed the role in June 1421, but was summoned to France again in April 1422, to be replaced once more by Gloucester.

The keepers were responsible for the routine government of the realm, presiding over parliaments in the king's absence. They were also in charge of the defence of the borders with Scotland and control of Wales. Henry reserved for himself all other matters to do with international relations, prerogative and grace (promotions, rewards and pardons) and handling petitions. He sent a barrage of peremptory commands from saddle and camp. No matter was too small to escape his attention, be it a payment of annuities, ordering restitution for an act of piracy or supervising the treatment of his prisoners in England. There was no doubt in anyone's mind who was ruling England, even if he were on the banks of the Seine.

Particularly distinctive was the king's use of English in correspondence sent under his privy seal. English had been used from time to time in official records since the reign of Edward III, but the language of government and the law was predominantly Latin and French. Henry's adoption of English when in France was deliberate, and many letters were in his own dictated words. Among his correspondence were reports designed for public consumption: news bulletins. The war was presented as a great national struggle bringing glory to the motherland. Other bodies and corporations followed his regal example and began to keep records in English, 'our mother-tongue ... honourably enlarged and adorned',[17] as one London livery company proudly noted.

Henry's deputies were successful in protecting his rear while he was campaigning. The attempts of the Duke of Albany to recover Roxburgh and Berwick, English outposts in Scotland, were decisively repulsed by Bedford in the autumn of 1417. Thereafter the Wardens of the Marches, the Earls of Northumberland (restored in 1416) and Westmorland, held the Scots in check, and even started taking the war to them.

Wales, too, was kept firmly under control. On becoming king, Henry had initiated a policy of reconciliation: pardons were offered to all remaining rebels if they would submit and commissions were established to enquire into abuses by his own officers (though communities were still required to purchase the king's grace with large fines). Many Welsh were even recruited into the king's armies – a phenomenon made immortal by Shakespeare in his none too flattering portrait of the common soldiers Fluellen and Williams. From 1415 Owain Glyn Dŵr disappears from the English record – although in later Welsh legend he never died. His sole surviving son, Maredudd, finally made his peace in 1421.

Sir John Oldcastle was still at large when Henry sailed to France in 1417, but he was eventually tracked down in Wales and captured. He was brought before parliament, condemned and executed that December. Lollards were still considered a threat, the occasional suspect being arrested and tried. Ireland was subjected to the ruthless rule of John Talbot, Lord Furnival, which ensured that there would be no danger from that quarter. Thus was England kept secure for Henry in his absence.

Henry's relations with the Church were more fraught. For two years, as the Council of Constance struggled to resolve the Great Schism, no pope was recognised officially, so Henry in effect governed the Church in England as well as the secular realm. Pope Martin V, elected in November 1417 with English support, attempted to reassert his authority over appointments. In return for papal support for Henry's cause in France, he put pressure on the king to repeal the Statute of Provisors and Praemunire, under which the exercise of papal authority in England had been restricted. Henry would have none of it.

In particular he was incensed at the behaviour of Henry Beaufort. Beaufort had been sent to the Council of Constance as the king's envoy in 1416. He had, on the king's instructions, swung the English delegation to support the election of a new pope prior to addressing the question of reform, thus abandoning the German position championed by King Sigismund. The pope was willing, as a reward, for Beaufort to be promoted to cardinal. Martin V went one step further, however, and made him his legate *a latere*, with full papal authority over the affairs of the Church in England and exemption from the jurisdiction of Canterbury. Henry was furious. Beaufort was threatened with the full force of the Act of Praemunire, which forbade the acceptance of papal promotion without royal approval. For two years he was out of royal favour. Eventually he made his peace: a reconciliation marked in 1421 by the grant of a huge loan to the king. Henry would neither tolerate the insubordination of his closest adviser, nor allow for a moment any challenge to his de facto control over the Church within his realm.

Henry used his control of the Church not only to secure his own promotions and appointments to high office but also to advance his personal programme of monastic reform. This was partly propagated through his own monastic foundations set up in the first year of his reign and clustered around his royal estate at Sheen, west of London. These were new orders which adhered to strict and austere rules. In 1421, when he was back in England briefly, he took on the reform of the wealthy and somewhat lax Benedictine order as well. He urged a meeting of monastic representatives to tighten their discipline and drew up proposals for closer observance of their rule. His suggestions were quietly rejected, however, and more modest proposals adopted. The Black Monks went largely on their comfortable way.

Henry's attempt to initiate monastic reform occurred during the meeting of parliament and convocation in May 1421. Eleven separate parliaments were held during his reign, an average of more than one a year. Four were held in his absence. As Prince of Wales he had learnt the necessity of managing the Commons. All the Speakers elected by MPs were king's men, and a solid phalanx of MPs returned to the House at every election backed the Crown. Nobles exercised patronage in their counties to secure such support. The Beaufort bloc, for instance – often a dozen or so strong – was managed by Sir Thomas Chaucer, the poet's son, who was the Speaker five times between 1407 and 1421.

The Crown may have been able to mobilise a party of King's Friends in the House, but it did not always have its own way. A short parliament in December 1420, with Gloucester presiding, truculently requested that future sittings should no longer be held in the king's absence, and that parliament's bills should be answered in England in person, not by the king somewhere in France. It also insisted (with the Treaty of Troyes in mind) that an assurance given by Edward III in 1340, that his people would never be subject to French law, be reissued.

MPs responded to their electors, and the electorate, though not yet formally defined in the counties, included many folk of modest means from whose ranks the archers of the king's armies were recruited, and who bore the principal burden of direct taxation. For seven years they voted Henry's government unprecedented sums. The victories won by the king, the tangible benefits of greater security at home and on the borders, the potential winnings to be made in France and the stimulus of government spending to the economy made him a popular monarch. But by 1420 the taxpayers were beginning to feel that they had paid enough. The tax take from the beginning of the reign (and concentrated between 1414 and 1419) averaged over £100,000 a year. Signs of resistance to these payments emerged in Cheshire in 1416, even though it was then a royal palatinate. By 1421 the royal finances were in deficit and many of the crown jewels had to be pledged in order to sustain the war. That spring the king resorted, in effect, to a forced loan. In Lincolnshire, and no doubt elsewhere, he commanded, ominously, that the names be taken of those who declined to lend.

The remorseless search for money led Henry to the rapacious exploitation of legal technicalities in an effort to swell his coffers – a practice later followed by Henry VII. Many of his subjects were caught out in this way, particularly widows who found their property confiscated because their husbands had not been careful enough in their will provision. The unfortunate Beatrice, Lady Talbot, widow of one of Henry's oldest and most loyal companions in arms who had died during the siege of Rouen, was Portuguese. Her husband had failed to take out appropriate letters of denizenship for her. All the inheritance, not just her dower, were seized by the exchequer. She was not allowed to reclaim it until she had agreed to pay a fine of over £1,500. The king's stepmother, Joan of Navarre, was even more disgracefully treated. In October 1419 he ordered her arrest on the trumped-up charge of sorcery so that he could confiscate her dower worth £6,000 per annum. (He may also have resented his stepmother personally: a widow herself, she had married his father in what was almost certainly a love match in 1403.)

The king's increasingly heavy rule was driven not only by financial need, but by a continuing fear of challenges to the throne. His concern at times bordered on paranoia. He would not let the Earl of March, whom he took to France, lead a normal, independent life befitting a man of his station. An obscure and probably illegitimate member of the earl's family, Sir John Mortimer, who had served the king in war since 1415, was arrested and imprisoned in 1418 on the accusation of uttering seditious words. In April 1422, after a failed attempt to escape from the Tower, he was arraigned for treason on the grounds that an escape from prison while facing a charge of treason was itself an act of treason. There were signs that Henry was beginning to behave despotically. It was a tendency spotted by Adam of Usk in the last words he wrote in his chronicle in May 1421 about the forced loans to finance the king's forthcoming return to France:

> The lord king is now fleecing everyone with any money, rich or poor, throughout the realm ... No

wonder, then, that the unbearable impositions being demanded from the people … are accompanied by dark – though private – mutterings and curses, and by hatred of such extortions: and I pray that my supreme lord may not in the end like Julius (and others) incur the sword of the Lord's fury.[18]

It is doubtful that Henry V would have suffered Caesar's fate, but his early death certainly came in time to save his reputation from the imputation of tyranny.

9

'We in it shall be remembered':
Apotheosis and Reputation[19]

Henry V's body was returned to England in solemn state. Having been embalmed and placed inside a double coffin (wood encased in lead), it was carried in funeral process to St Denis, where a Requiem Mass was sung. It was then transported by water to Rouen, where the dead king lay in state for two weeks. The cortège left Rouen on 5 October 1422 and moved slowly north to Calais, passing close by the scene of his greatest triumph. (En route, news arrived of the death on 21 October of Charles VI.) Not until 5 November did Henry's body arrive in London, where it was received by a carefully orchestrated display of collective mourning in which each member of every guild wore a black hood and provided candles for the processional route. The last of many Requiem Masses was celebrated in Westminster Abbey where the coffin was finally interred on 7 November. Had he lived seven weeks longer, Henry V of England would have become Henri II of France.

Before he died Henry had made dispositions for his body, soul and kingdom, adding codicils to his will. He ordered the singing of a large number of Masses for his soul and for the forgiveness of his sins. He made lavish bequests to his newly founded religious houses and provided for a chantry chapel to be built near the tomb of St Edward in Westminster Abbey. Gifts were distributed to his closest servants. The tutelage of his heir, now Henry VI, was entrusted to Thomas Beaufort, Duke of Exeter. It would take his executors, including the now fully restored Bishop of Winchester, twenty years to settle all his debts, and longer to fulfil all the terms of the will.

Henry's tomb in Westminster Abbey was constructed of finest Purbeck marble. It took until 1431 to complete his effigy. The chantry chapel – the mausoleum built to Henry's own design – was not finished until 1450. Elaborately carved in the perpendicular style, it resembled a fortified gateway about to be stormed – the gateway to Heaven, no doubt. Every year, on the anniversary of his death, Masses were to be sung for the success of this, his final campaign. It became a shrine to his memory, and the focus also for an annual celebration to which the monks invited the great and good of the land. For a while Henry's memory was also honoured in celebrations of Agincourt Day, and, more lastingly, on the feast of St George, which he had made a two-day national celebration. St George had emerged as one of the pre-eminent national saints in the fourteenth century; however, by his emphasis and use of the familiar red cross on a white background in his banners and on his uniforms, it was Henry who turned him into *the* patron saint of England.

Henry V's dispositions for the ruling of the kingdom were not followed to the letter. He had declared in his will that the elder of his surviving brothers, John, Duke of Bedford, should become Regent of France, on the accession of Henry VI as heir to the thrones of England

and France. His brother Gloucester was nominated Regent of England. There was no issue over France, but once the dead king had been buried, the new ruling council, backed by Bedford, determined that it was unconstitutional for there to be a regent in England. Thus Gloucester was made Protector of the Realm and president of a standing council which would rule England with collective responsibility.

At first, devotion to the late monarch's memory ensured the smooth running of the kingdom, but by 1424 tensions began to emerge – especially in an increasingly bitter rivalry between Gloucester and Henry Beaufort, who finally gained his cardinal's hat in 1426. Personal animosities notwithstanding, the council kept faith with the memory of the dead king so as to pass on his inheritance to his son when he came of age. Henry VI was educated by two of the noblest exemplars of chivalry and most renowned of Henry V's captains, Thomas Beaufort, Duke of Exeter, and, following his death in 1426, Richard Beauchamp, Earl of Warwick. Their intention was the forging of another Christian warrior. Unfortunately, Henry VI absorbed only the Christian part: he rejected war. Once he had come of age, after 1437, his slack rule permitted descent into faction and ultimately his own deposition in 1461.

In France, under Bedford's vigorous and fresh leadership, English fortunes revived. Two significant victories were won in the field: at Cravant in 1423, when a dauphinist advance on Burgundy was checked by the Earl of Salisbury, and, more emphatically, at Verneuil in 1424, when Bedford decisively rebuffed a major assault by the dauphin's army on Normandy. Thereafter the English conquest was extended, particularly to the south. It was, however, impossible to sustain the war effort in the longer term and to make a reality of Henry VI's throne in France. Following the dramatic intervention of Joan of Arc in 1429, Charles VIII was crowned King of France at Rheims. His position was further strengthened in 1435 when he came to terms with Philip, Duke of Burgundy, who abandoned the English alliance.

It was then only a matter of time before the English either accepted a humiliating peace or were expelled completely from the land in which Henry V had made his conquests. In the end, no peace treaty agreeable to both sides could be found. The English tenaciously held on to Normandy for a further fifteen years but had to concede defeat eventually. More disastrous still, Aquitaine was also lost. The year was 1453. All that Henry V had won a generation earlier, all that the English Crown had held in France for 300 years – everything bar Calais – was lost. Eight years later England too was lost to the house of Lancaster.

At its first formal meeting in November 1422, the minority council of Henry VI minuted an epitaph for its dead hero: 'The most Christian warrior of the Church, the sun of prudence, the exemplar of justice, the most invincible King, and the flower of Chivalry.'[20] These were the conventional virtues of the ideal monarch – those upon which Henry V had fashioned himself. This image dominated the representations of him for years to come, becoming ever more embedded as his kingdoms fell apart.

Henry was fortunate in his early historians. They wrote in the euphoria of his victories. Unusually among late medieval kings of England, he was, with the notable exception of Adam of Usk, beloved of clerical writers. The household chaplain who wrote the *Gesta Henrici Quinti* in 1417 established the image of the Christian warrior waging a holy war, with divine providence on his side. Other monastic authors, including Walsingham, were deeply impressed by his austere, ascetic lifestyle. Henry's youngest brother Humphrey, who idolised him, commissioned a life in about 1438 by the Italian humanist Tito Livio, which reinforced the notion of a chivalric hero, while also urging Gloucester's countrymen to keep up the good fight. This portrait entered the mainstream of historical writing, carried in both the London chronicles and the popular history of England known as *The Brut* (so called because it begins with the legendary Brutus, founder of Britain).

Henry's enemies respected (as well as feared) him as an exemplar of chivalry. The historian of the royal abbey of St Denis in Paris, Walsingham's French counterpart, noted that the king was courteous, behaved entirely properly with his noble prisoners, was pitiless to those who defied him, but fair to those who obeyed him. If he had a sin, the commentator averred, it was pride. Later French historians, writing in the mid-fifteenth century, likewise stressed Henry's chivalric credentials, but they introduced a sharper tone. He had ruled by fear, they said, and his wrath was dreaded by English and French alike. As Jean de

Waurin wrote, 'he punished with death without any mercy those who disobeyed or infringed his commands'.[21]

The Yorkist kings, though they disparaged the Lancastrian dynasty as usurpers, made an exception of Henry because of his triumphs overseas and did nothing to diminish his standing. When he came to the throne on 1509, the young Henry VIII hoped to emulate his namesake and predecessor by winning glory in France. And although history repeated itself as farce, he sponsored a new edition and translation of Tito Livio's *Vita*. All sixteenth-century historians followed along the established lines, culminating in Shakespeare's plays (though *Henry V*, for all its jingoism, does not hesitate to reveal the horrors of war). And so it continued through the seventeenth and eighteenth centuries into the nineteenth. There was one fixed view of Henry as the great warrior and quintessential English hero.

In the nineteenth century, essayists and antiquaries, perhaps reflecting war weariness after the defeat of Napoleon, began for the first time to introduce a new critical tone. William Hazlitt tartly commented in 1817 (*Characters of Shakespeare's Plays*) that Henry might have been a hero for his willingness to sacrifice his own life for the pleasure of destroying thousands of others. Others took up the theme that Henry's wars were wanton acts of aggression. Debate was joined by William Stubbs in 1878, who reasserted the traditional view, but adding an imperial gloss: his Henry was a true Englishman, who 'made England the first power in Europe',[22] a theme followed by C.L. Kingsford in the first modern, research-based biography, published in 1901. This work also reflected the revival of Victorian chivalry, in picturing him as the true type of medieval hero king in pursuit of a great ideal.

Thus were the foundations laid for the debate which has run through all writings on Henry V over the last hundred years. On one side he has been characterised as the greatest of England's monarchs; a national hero; the exemplification of the chivalric ideal; the man who came closer than any other to embodying the contemporary vision of the just king; a ruler who possessed all the characteristics expected of a medieval monarch and more – a charismatic leader, a brilliant soldier and a gifted administrator. On the other hand, he has been described as a fanatic, cruel – sadistic even – sanctimonious, priggish, overbearingly proud, a hypocrite and a ruthless war criminal whose conquests were futile and whose legacy was divisive. Perhaps, not surprisingly, modern French historians have tended to concur with this second version.

The lines of debate are clear. Historians who admire Henry V tend to stress that he should be seen only in the terms of his own world, of his own culture of Christian chivalry and of the codes by which he and his contemporaries lived: it is no part of the historian's craft to apply modern criteria and values. Critics tend to be sceptical of the construction of the king as the model monarch, seeing in it the work of a skilled mythmaker. They are also more willing to apply modern attitudes to war and peace, justice and religion.

In this respect, it is worth remembering that history is an ever-moving dialogue between past and present. No one can avoid approaching the past from the point of view of their own age and its values. In the late nineteenth century, Henry V was envisaged as an exemplar of muscular Christianity, the model for youths about to embark on imperial service. Some of the most enthusiastic words in his praise in the twentieth century were written during or shortly after the First and Second World Wars. His appeal as a national hero endures for those who delight in the martial deeds of charismatic leaders, who regret the passing of imperial might and who yearn for the 'Great' to be put back in Britain.

Productions of Shakespeare's totemic play reflect this constantly shifting discourse about England's greatness, just war, aggression and atrocity. Laurence Olivier's renowned film, made as part of the British war effort, cut out the passage in which the king swears to let loose his soldiers on Harfleur's 'fresh fair virgins' and 'flowering infants', for 'hot and forcing violation'.[23] In 1944 only Nazis did that sort of thing. Kenneth Branagh's 1989 version stressed the grim reality of war, setting Agincourt in the mud rather than on a sunny plain. Nicholas Hytner's modern-dress production at the National Theatre in 2003 provided a no-holds-barred anti-war reading, complete with massacres of innocent civilians, executions of prisoners and 'dodgy dossiers'. Productions of Shakespeare's play may reflect more overtly the modern political agenda, but historical studies inevitably engage with the same themes.

10

'This star of England':
Assessment[24]

From contemporary reports and images one can gain a sense of what Henry V looked like. His appearance was commanding. He was said to be of above average height for his age, slim but strong. His face and nose were long, though no doubt disfigured from the age of 16 by the scar he had acquired at Shrewsbury. No one mentioned the scar; we only know of it from the surgeon's report, but we can imagine that it might have reinforced the sense of him as brave and even fearsome. His hair was cut short and high above his ears. He was clean shaven. If the head carved on the rood screen at York Minster not long after his death is a likeness, he may have grown a beard after his marriage.

His words, we are told, were few and well chosen. He was courteous and a stickler for etiquette and protocol. He was short tempered. He was haughty and proud. As the mid-fifteenth-century Burgundian chronicler Enguerrand de Monstrelet reported, he would not allow anyone who came into his presence to look him in the face. He was well educated and able to read Latin. He had a fine collection of books and was a patron of poets. He was musical: it seems likely he played the harp and may have been the 'Roy Henry' who composed a couple of pieces for the royal chapel.

We cannot doubt that he was a man of exceptional energy, ability and magnetism. He was an outstanding general, having learnt in his adolescence that armies marched on their stomachs, that wars were won by discipline and that exemplary terror was highly effective. He understood that attention to detail and logistics was as important as a grasp of strategy and tactics. He was an inspiring leader of men, who led by example and frequently put his own body in harm's way. In later years, he was a consummate politician, managing his key subjects at court and parliament with a deft hand. He inspired devotion and loyalty from his followers, fear and dread in his enemies. He understood the arts of persuasion and image making. His slogan, 'the end of war is peace', would have delighted any twentieth-century dictator. In this sense he was a master of 'spin'. His reign was a public performance, acted out with close attention to the script of *The Mirrors for Princes*, the manual for model medieval rulers with which contemporaries were familiar. He had a clear and deliberate sense of how best to represent himself for public consumption. And it all went down exceedingly well with his jingoistic subjects.

After his accession to the throne the man concealed himself behind the actor's mask of office. Only occasionally, as in the treatment of the Southampton plotters, did something of the young man who had been Prince of Wales emerge. For all his claims to uphold justice, he bent the law when it suited him, either in crushing opponents or extorting money. He knew how to exploit any dissent to suggest a plot against him and he appreciated the value of show trials. As his reign progressed he became increasingly tyrannical. Henry V was not unique among English medieval kings in this or indeed among dictators throughout history. The snow on the day he was crowned did indeed portend that he would be a king of 'cold deeds, severe in the management of his kingdom'.[25]

Henry's court, at least until his marriage in 1420, was an exclusively male world; his coterie of like-minded chivalric, young alpha males shared the camaraderie of the locker room and were eager to perform feats of arms on the field of battle. He was a man not known for his liking of or generosity towards women – as his stepmother discovered. The code of conduct laid down for his army not only prohibited prostitutes within 2 miles of the camp, but also forbade garrison men from cohabiting with any but their wives. Above all, his ideal was monastic. Clean shaven like a priest, he perhaps shared with the priestly order some of its misogyny. Indeed, one witness described him as being more like a priest in demeanour than a soldier. The *Gesta Henrici Quinti* supplies a unique insight into his image of himself as 'the elect of God',[26] doing all he could to promote the Church as well as to secure a final peace and reconciliation of the two kingdoms of England and France. He bathed himself in an aura of sanctity. He behaved with the increasing conviction that if he did something it was *ipso facto* right; if necessary the law and evidence could be modified to justify his actions. In this respect, he was that most dangerous of all leaders: one who had absolute confidence in his own righteousness.

In war he could be violently unforgiving. We have seen how the prisoners were slaughtered at Agincourt, how reprisals were taken, how exemplary punishment was inflicted on those who resisted or turned their coats. He could also be vindictive: at the surrender of Meaux he demanded that a trumpeter, who had mocked him from the walls by imitating the braying of a donkey, be handed over for execution. We should recall, however, that others among his contemporaries also committed atrocities, and some – John the Fearless, for example – were far worse.

Moreover, vengeance was validated by the code of chivalry. The murder of prisoners, the taking of reprisals, the wanton destruction of cities were acceptable actions, provided the appropriate protocols or laws of war were followed. The significant difference between massacres, atrocities and the use of terror in the modern and medieval worlds is that the court of world opinion today tends to condemn without exception where once it was wont to condone in specific circumstances. Thus Henry's cruelty has often been excused by modern opinion on the grounds that it was acceptable in his own day.

The inescapable truth is that Henry V was a warmonger. His slogan, relentlessly hammered throughout his reign, was disingenuous. In reality, the end of war was not peace; it was more war. Adam of Usk, as well as condemning his extortions, feared that 'the money of the kingdom will be miserably wasted'.[27] And so it proved. It has been argued that Lydgate's *Troy Book* (1412–20) and *Siege of Thebes* (*c.* 1422) are coded anti-imperialist, anti-war tracts, warning Henry V against aggression in the spurious name of peace. If so, here is further indication that not all his subjects were persuaded of the wisdom, justice or virtue of his cause.

Henry seemed not to grasp that, unless he negotiated with a united France, the final peace he claimed to be pursuing would forever elude him. The Treaty of Troyes was an alliance between two parties in a civil war designed to destroy a third. It did more to continue than to conclude the conflict. His claim to have ended it was mere sophistry. It might be argued that by surrendering his Plantagenet claim in exchange for his adoption as a Valois, he secured the best deal available. It cannot be convincingly suggested that he should alternatively have renounced the claim and settled for the implementation of Brétigny: that would not have lasted. But he never considered offering himself as a mediator, a true peacemaker, a role which, with suitable concessions, might have bought a period of proper respite. The plain conclusion is that there was no prospect of a lasting peace on the basis of an English victory – and Henry never wanted peace except through unconditional surrender. He had no other exit strategy. For a moment, Henry V towered over his contemporaries and his fame spread throughout all Christendom. But his ultimate legacy was the bankrupting of his realm and the destruction of his dynasty. His ambition was, quite simply, too gigantic.

Henry V's Portrait

The National Portrait Gallery image of Henry V, a later copy, is unique among portrayals of fifteenth-century kings of England in that it is shown in profile. This may be because of the scar he carried from the Battle of Shrewsbury. Federico Montefeltro, Duke of Urbino, was also portrayed in profile because he had lost his right eye. John Bradmore, the surgeon who removed the arrowhead, wrote that Henry was struck in the face beside the nose on the left side. But Henry is shown from the left side – the side upon which he was wounded – though no scar is shown. Bradmore might have meant the left side as he looked at the face, i.e. the right cheek, but this seems unlikely. Has a copyist reversed the portrait? Richard II was portrayed in profile in the Wilton Dyptych. Could this pose have been adopted in homage to Henry's cousin?

Whatever the explanation, the scar is not shown.

Please see the back cover for depiction of this portrait.

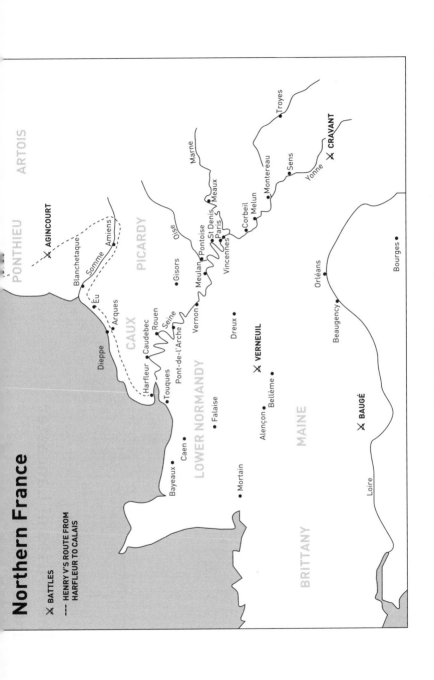

Northern France

✗ BATTLES

--- HENRY V'S ROUTE FROM
    HARFLEUR TO CALAIS

ARTOIS

PONTHIEU

✗ AGINCOURT

Blanchetaque

Somme   Amiens

Eu

Arques

Dieppe

CAUX

PICARDY

Harfleur   Caudebec
         Rouen
Touques Seine
   Pont-de-l'Arche

Vernon

Gisors

Oise

Meulan
Pontoise
St Denis
Paris   Meaux
Vincennes

Marne

Corbeil
Melun
Montereau

Sens

Troyes

Yonne

✗ CRAVANT

LOWER NORMANDY

Dreux

✗ VERNEUIL

Bayeaux

Caen

Falaise

Alençon   Bellème

Mortain

MAINE

Orléans

Beaugency

Bourges

✗ BAUGÉ

BRITTANY

Loire

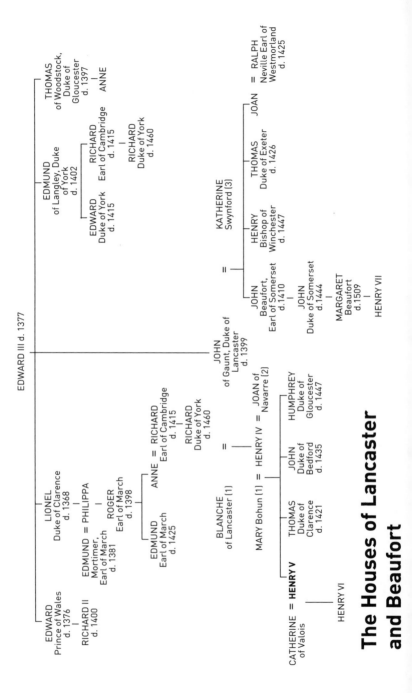

EDWARD III d. 1377

EDWARD
Prince of Wales
d. 1376
|
RICHARD II
d. 1400

LIONEL
Duke of Clarence
d. 1368
|
EDMUND = PHILIPPA
Mortimer,
Earl of March
d. 1381

ROGER
Earl of March
d. 1398

EDMUND
Earl of March
d. 1425

ANNE = RICHARD
Earl of Cambridge
d. 1415
|
RICHARD
Duke of York
d. 1460

JOHN
of Gaunt, Duke of
Lancaster
d. 1399

EDMUND
of Langley, Duke
of York
d. 1402

EDWARD
Duke of York
d. 1415

RICHARD
Earl of Cambridge
d. 1415
|
RICHARD
Duke of York
d. 1460

THOMAS
of Woodstock,
Duke of
Gloucester
d. 1397
|
ANNE

BLANCHE
of Lancaster [1]

MARY Bohun [1] = HENRY IV = JOAN of
Navarre [2]

THOMAS
Duke of
Clarence
d. 1421

JOHN
Duke of
Bedford
d. 1435

HUMPHREY
Duke of
Gloucester
d. 1447

CATHERINE = **HENRY V**
of Valois

HENRY VI

KATHERINE
Swynford [3]

=

JOHN
Beaufort,
Earl of Somerset
d. 1410

JOHN
Duke of Somerset
d. 1444

MARGARET
Beaufort
d. 1509
|
HENRY VII

HENRY
Bishop of
Winchester
d. 1447

THOMAS
Duke of Exeter
d. 1426

JOAN = RALPH
Neville Earl of
Westmorland
d. 1425

The Houses of Lancaster and Beaufort

Notes

1 Shakespeare, William, *Henry VI Part 1*, act I, scene i, line 15.
2 Shakespeare, William, *Henry IV Part 1*, act I, scene i, line 80.
3 Ibid., act I, scene i, line 85.
4 Shakespeare, William, *Henry IV Part 2*, act V, scene v, line 61.
5 Taylor, F. & Roskell, J.S. (ed. & trans.), *Gesta Henrici Quinti* (Clarendon Press, 1975), p. 3.
6 Prest, David (trans.), *The Chronica Maiora of Thomas Walsingham, 1376–1422* (Boydell Press, 2005), p. 389.
7 Brie, F.W. (ed.), *The Brut or Chronicles of England*, ii (London, 1908), pp. 594–5.
8 Hearne, T. (ed.), *Vita et Gesta Henrici Quinti* (1727), p. 12.
9 Marx, William (ed.), *An English Chronicle, 1377–1461* (Boydell Press, 2003), p. 42.
10 Shakespeare, William, *Henry V*, act II, chorus, line 3.
11 Given-Wilson, C., et al. (eds) *The Parliament Rolls of Medieval England* (Leicester, 2005), CD version, November 1414, 2.
12 *Henry V*, op. cit., act III, scene i, line 32.

13 Ibid., act III, scene i, line 1.

14 *The Brut or Chronicles of England*, ii, op. cit., p. 410.

15 *Henry V*, op. cit., prologue, line 11.

16 Ibid., act IV, scene iii, line 64.

17 London, Guildhall Library, Ms 5440.

18 Given-Wilson, C. (ed. & trans.), *The Chronicle of Adam of Usk, 1377–1421* (Clarendon Press, 1997), p. 271.

19 *Henry V*, op. cit., act IV, scene iii, line 59.

20 Nicolas, N.H., *Proceeding and Ordinances of the Privy Council of England* (7 vols, 1834–37), vol. 3, p. 3.

21 de Waurin, Jehan, *Receuil des cronicques et anchiennes istoires de la Grant Bretaignee* (5 vols, Rolls Series, 1864–91), vol. 2, p. 391.

22 Stubbs, William, *Constitutional History of England* (1878), vol. 3, pp. 74, 77.

23 *Henry V*, op. cit., act III, scene iii, lines 14, 20–1.

24 Ibid., epilogue, line 6.

25 *Chronica Maiora of Thomas Walsingham, 1376–1422*, op. cit., p. 389.

26 *Gesta Henrici Quinti*, op. cit., p. 3.

27 *The Chronicle of Adam of Usk, 1377–1421*, op. cit., p. 271.

Glossary

Lollardy

The name given to the heresy inspired by the teachings of John Wycliffe (d. 1384), which in several ways prefigured Protestantism

Praemunire

A process enshrined in English law which imposed penalties on anyone who secured appointment by the papacy in England against royal wishes

Taxation

The laity paid both direct and indirect taxes to the Crown. Direct taxation was in the form of a subsidy voted by parliament, which was one-fifteenth of the moveable wealth of country people, one-tenth of townsfolk. After 1334 these had been levied communally, vill (land unit) by vill, on the basis of an assessment made in 1332. Each settlement determined who contributed to its levy. They were collected in instalments. Indirect taxation was raised on wool exports, exports and imports of general goods (poundage) and on imports of wine (tunnage). Parliament voted these to Henry V for life in 1415. The clergy were taxed on some of their property at the rate of a tenth voted from time to time by convocation

Timeline

1386	16 September: birth of Prince Henry at Monmouth
1394	4 June: death of Henry's mother, Mary de Bohun
1398	16 September: exile of Henry's father, Henry Bolingbroke, Duke of Hereford; Henry's twelfth birthday
1399	3 February: death of John of Gaunt, Duke of Lancaster, Henry V's grandfather
	30 September: abdication of Richard II
	13 October: coronation of Henry IV
	15 October: creation of Henry of Monmouth as Prince of Wales, Duke of Cornwall and Earl of Chester
1400	July–September: invasion of Scotland
	September: Owain Glyn Dŵr's rebellion
1401	April–May: first campaign in Wales for relief of Conwy
1403	7 March: created Lieutenant of Wales for first time
	21 July: Battle of Shrewsbury
1405	May: rising of Archbishop Scrope of York

1406	January: reappointed Lieutenant of Wales
	April: onset of Henry IV's chronic illness
	8 December: Prince of Wales nominated to
	governing council
1407	July–October: abortive siege of Aberystwyth
1408	July–November: second, successful siege of
	Aberystwyth
1409	December: fall of Arundel ministry
1410	January: formation of ministry under Prince
	of Wales
1411	October: Earl of Arundel's expedition to
	France
	December: fall of Prince of Wales ministry,
	return of Arundel and Prince Thomas
1412	June: Prince of Wales first armed
	demonstration against government
	August: second armed demonstration
1413	21 March: accession of Henry V
	9 April: coronation of Heny V
	December: reburial of Richard II
1414	11 January: Oldcastle Rising
	July: dispatch of first embassy to France
	November: declaration in parliament of
	intention to invade France
1415	February: foundation of Syon Abbey
	April: foundation of Sheen Charterhouse
	1 August: Southampton Plot
	11 August: opening of siege of Harfleur
	22 September: surrender of Harfleur

	25 October: Battle of Agincourt
	23 November: London triumph
1416	2 May: arrival in England of Sigismund, King of the Romans
	15 August: Battle of the Seine; Treaty of Canterbury with King Sigismund
	3–13 October: Calais summit between Henry V, Sigismund and Duke of Burgundy
1417	29 June: Battle of Cap de le Hève
	1 August: landing of second expedition on beaches of Normandy
	4 September: surrender of Caen
1418	14 February: fall of Falaise
	31 July: opening of siege of Rouen
1419	19 January: fall of Rouen
	June–July: negotiations between Henry V and Burgundians at Meulan
	30 July: capture of Pontoise
	10 September: assassination of John the Fearless at Montereau
1420	21 May: Treaty of Troyes
	2 June: marriage of Henry V and Catherine of France
	1 July: fall of Montereau
	July–November: siege of Melun
1421	1 February: return of Henry and Catherine to England
	23 February: coronation of Queen Catherine
	22 March: Battle of Beaugé

	10 June: return of Henry V to France
	6 October: opening of siege of Meaux
	6 December: birth of Henry VI
1422	10 May: fall of Meaux
	31 August: death of Henry V
	24 October: death of Charles VI of France
	7 November: burial of Henry V in Westminster Abbey
1450	Completion of Henry V's mausoleum in Westminster Abbey; final loss of Normandy

Further Reading

Allmand, C.T., *Henry V* (Methuen, 1992)

Allmand, C.T., *Lancastrian Normandy, 1415–1450* (Clarendon Press, 1983)

Barker, Juliet, *Conquest: The English Kingdom of France in the Hundred Years War* (Little Brown, 2009)

Curry, Anne, 'After Agincourt, What Next? Henry V and the Campaign of 1416', in Clark, Linda (ed.), *The Fifteenth Century, VII, Conflicts, Consequences and the Crown in the Late Middle Ages* (Boydell and Brewer, 2007)

Curry, Anne, *Agincourt: A New History* (Tempus, 2005)

Davies, R.R., *The Revolt of Owain Glyn Dŵr* (Oxford University Press, 1995)

Dockray, Keith, *Henry V* (Tempus, 2004)

Dodd, Gwilym (ed.), *Henry V: New Interpretations* (Boydell and Brewer, 2013)

Given-Wilson, C. (ed. & trans.), *The Chronicle of Adam of Usk, 1377–1421* (Clarendon Press, 1997)

Harriss, G.L. (ed.), *Henry V: The Practice of Kingship* (Oxford University Press, 1985)

Harriss, G.L., *Cardinal Beaufort* (Clarendon Press, 1988)

Kingsford, C.L., *Henry V: The Typical Medieval Hero* (Oxford University Press, 1901)

Lewis, Katherine J., *Kingship and Masculinity in Late Medieval England* (Routledge, 2013)

Matusiac, John, *Henry V* (Routledge, 2013)

Mortimer, Ian, *1415: Henry V's Year of Glory* (Bodley Head, 2009)

Pollard, A.J., *Late Medieval England, 1399–1509* (Longman, 2000)

Prest, David (trans.), *The Chronica Maiora of Thomas Walsingham, 1376–1422* (Boydell Press, 2005)

Pugh, T.B., *Henry V and the Southampton Plot* (Sutton, 1988)

Strohm, Paul, *England's Empty Throne: Usurpation and the Language of Legitimation, 1399–1422* (Yale University Press, 1998)

Taylor, F. & Roskell, J.S. (ed. & trans.), *Gesta Henrici Quinti* (Clarendon Press, 1975)

Vaughan, Richard, *John the Fearless: The Growth of Burgundian Power* (Longman, 1966)

Acknowledgements

I was commissioned to write a short life that was opinionated and 'with attitude'. I hope I have not disappointed in that respect and have not upset too many of my colleagues as a result. They know that I am not a great admirer of Henry of Monmouth. The format, which reduces the scholarly apparatus to a minimum, does not allow me to acknowledge their work as directly as I would have liked. Many of them, who are contributors to a collection of new essays on Henry V edited by Gwilym Dodd, will recognise the borrowed line, the lifted detail, the sentiment here or the slant there. Thank you. In addition, I would like to thank Keith Dockray for allowing me to plunder his survey of the historiography, Dick Kaeuper for giving me confidence to be blunt about chivalry, Tig Lang for putting me right on Henry V's facial wound and Tony Morris for twisting my arm.

Eryholme,
12 June 2013

Giuseppe Verdi Henry V **Brunel** Pope John Paul II **Jane Austen** William the Conqueror **Abraham Lincoln** Robert the Bruce **Charles Darwin** Buddha **Elizabeth I** Horatio Nelson **Wellington** Hannibal & Scipio **Jesus** Joan of Arc **Anne Frank** Alfred the Great **King Arthur** Henry Ford **Nelson Mandela**